Hidden
SCOTLAND

LAUREN MACCALLUM

T0306825

INTRODUCTION

Hidden Scotland isn't your typical Scottish travel guide; instead, this book aims to encourage you to define your own sense of adventure, to explore beyond the usual hotspots and get to know the real Scotland. This book invites you to adopt and embrace that unique Scottish state of mind. It will help you to see beyond the tartan trinkets, Irn-Bru and haggis, and to experience the authentic life in Scotland. You'll be able, so we hope, to genuinely connect with the land, the language and the culture, and to enjoy the magic in the music the people sing. Bring all of these ingredients together, and you'll understand what's so unique about this small stretch of land and its inhabitants. Naturally, this guide also lists some popular locations, but they are presented from a local's perspective.

It's important to know that Scotland is much more than the staged tourism of the Royal Mile: it's raw, complicated and fascinating. Scotland has a great story to tell, especially to those who are patient and willing to stop and listen. Travelling with this guide will make your visit worth your while, because Scotland has so much to offer. We hope the addresses, places and tips that were selected for this guide reflect that, and that the lists will give you a great place to start creating your own special memories.

This book doesn't tell you everything there is to do and see in Scotland, far from it. It's more like a list of suggestions on the back of a napkin, scribbled down by a friendly local you bumped into. Just bring your curiosity, your generosity and your enthusiasm. Scotland is waiting.

ABOUT THE AUTHOR

Lauren MacCallum has lived in every corner of Scotland. Over the past 20 years she has moved from Kinross to Aberdeen, Edinburgh, Glasgow and Fort William, to finally settle in Aviemore, in the heart of the Cairngorms National Park. She has spent many summers exploring the Kintyre area – she has strong family ties there. She is absolutely dedicated to the outdoor lifestyle, and loves to spend time in Scotland's mountains, glens and beaches.

Lauren has previously worked in the Snowsports and Cycling industry, and is currently General Manager of charity 'Protect Our Winters UK'. She's also a public speaker and TV presenter for BBC Scotland's *Adventure Show*.

Lauren is passionate about exploring new places, mountain biking, snowboarding, and music festivals; she loves speciality coffee as well as a good pint. Scotland is an excellent and unique place to enjoy all of those things, and much more.

Lauren would like to thank everyone who helped create this book and for trusting her with their favourite spots. Suggestions came from folks in the pub, friends, friends of friends, fellow outdoor enthusiasts and family. Thanks go to Matt Barr, Sam Mellish, and Bob Pia for helping me land the gig. And to Hammy Morison for letting her borrow his car in a time of need. Extra special thanks go to Lauren's loving family: without their support this book couldn't have been possible. And last but not least, to Dettie from Luster, who has to be the most patient woman in publishing.

HOW TO USE THIS BOOK

The idea behind this book is to list the places the author would recommend to a friend who was looking for a surprising destination or an unusual experience. It is different from other guidebooks in listing places by category rather than location. The maps in the beginning of the book, each representing a different region, allow you to put together a journey linking several hidden places. Or you can choose to concentrate on exploring just one region – each is a worthy travel destination in itself. A word of caution: the different regions on the maps in this book do not coincide with Scotland's official administrative districts.

Travelling to Scotland is easiest by boat or airplane (airports are in Glasgow, Edinburgh and Inverness). You'll find Scotland a great destination for a road trip. If you're travelling by car, be sure to mind the traffic regulations, especially those concerning the passing places. We advise you to halt regularly and to take your time for nice walks, adventurous hikes or breathtaking bike trips in the natural surroundings. If hiking and biking are your thing, you might not need a car at all, as you can reach the starting points of the major trails by bus or train. You'll find that there's a trail or walk for everyone; the Walking Highlands website is a very helpful source. Don't forget to bring along a map, because not all trails are (well) signposted.

Other great ways to get around in Scotland are by mountain bike, or you can go snowboarding in winter. And you should take a ferry a least once during your stay: a truly peaceful and at the same time adventurous experience.

DISCOVER MORE ONLINE

Hidden Scotland is part of the internationally successful travel guide series called *The 500 Hidden Secrets*. The series covers over 40 destinations and includes city guides, regional guides and guides that focus on a specific theme.

Curious about the other destinations? Or looking for inspiration for your next city trip? Visit THE500HIDDENSECRETS.COM. Here you can order every guide from our online shop and find tons of interesting travel content.

Also, don't forget to follow us on Instagram or Facebook for dreamy travel photos and ideas, as well as up-to-date information. Our socials are the easiest way to get in touch with us: we love hearing from you and appreciate all feedback.

the500hiddensecrets

@500hiddensecrets #500hiddensecrets

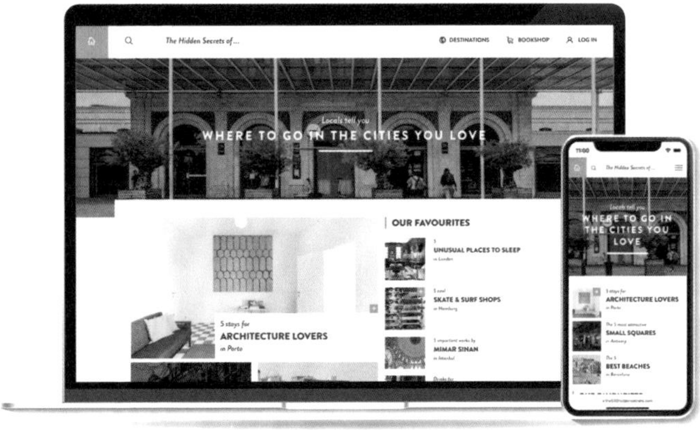

SCOTLAND

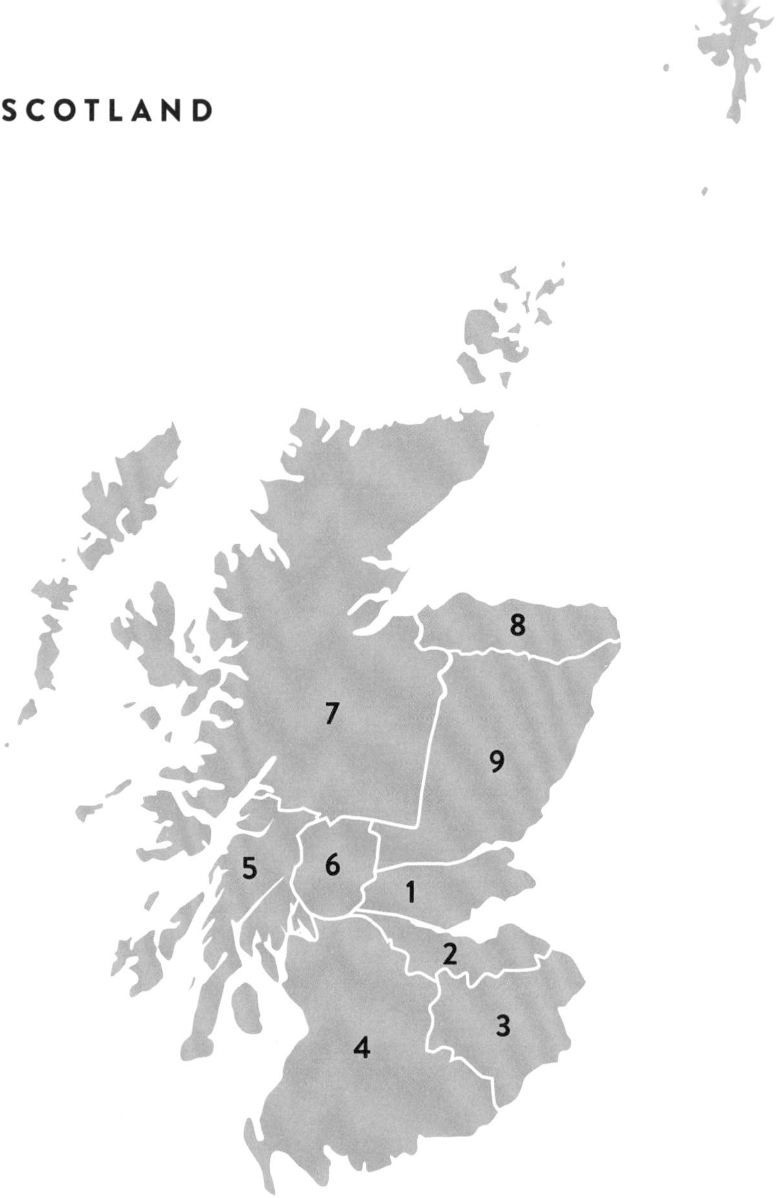

1 CENTRAL SCOTLAND

2 EDINBURGH & LOTHIANS

3 SCOTTISH BORDERS

4 GLASGOW & SOUTH

5 ARGYLL & BUTE

6 LOCH LOMOND & TROSSACHS

7 HIGHLANDS & ISLANDS

8 NORTH

9 NORTH EAST

1 CENTRAL SCOTLAND

#	ANSTRUTHER
90	Isle of May
177	Bowhouse Market, St Monans
185	Anstruther Fish Bar
279	The Murray Library Hostel
	CRIEFF
97	Comrie Croft, Braincroft
	CULROSS, FIFE
274	The Dundonald
	CUPAR
293	Dairsie Castle
	FALKLAND
207	Pillars of Hercules
	LEVEN, FIFE
100	Ruby Bay, Elie
	PERTH
52	Elcho Castle, Rhynd
160	Concorde Music
	PITTENWEEM
53	Kellie Castle
	ST ANDREWS
82	Eden Mill, Guardbridge
172	Kartel
193	Jannettas Gelateria

2 EDINBURGH & LOTHIANS

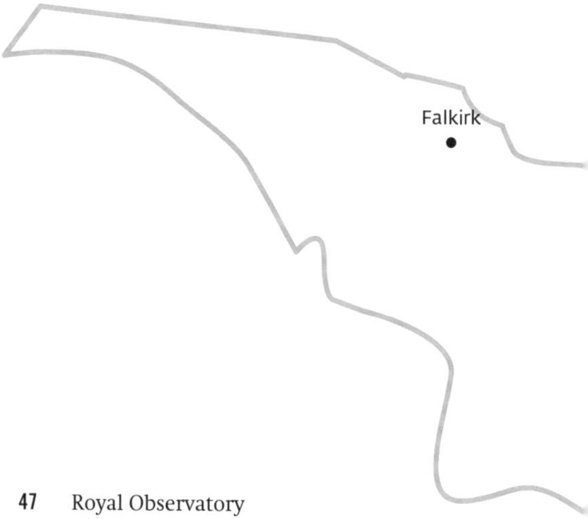

DUDDINGSTON VILLAGE

17 Dr Neil's Garden

DUNBAR

29 Belhaven Bridge
73 Victoria Harbour

EDINBURGH

1 Summerhall
9 Scottish National Gallery of Modern Art
10 Scottish National Portrait Gallery
15 National Museum of Scotland
18 Royal Botanic Garden Edinburgh
20 Calton Hill
24 Cramond Island
25 Water of Leith
31 Advocate's Close
41 Magdalen Chapel
43 National Archives of Scotland – General Register House
47 Royal Observatory Edinburgh
64 The Meadows
92 Gilmerton Cove
144 Armchair Books
148 Golden Hare Books
150 The Edinburgh Bookshop
158 W. Armstrong & Son
170 Dick's
176 I.J.Mellis
190 Over Langshaw Ice Cream
215 Gardener's Cottage
224 The Walnut
236 Little Fitzroy Coffee
237 Williams & Johnson Coffee Co.
238 Cairngorm Coffee
245 Cheap Shot Coffee
246 The Counter
252 Kay's Bar
253 Port O' Leith Bar
254 The Regent
255 Captain's Bar
256 The Royal Oak
262 The Royal Dick

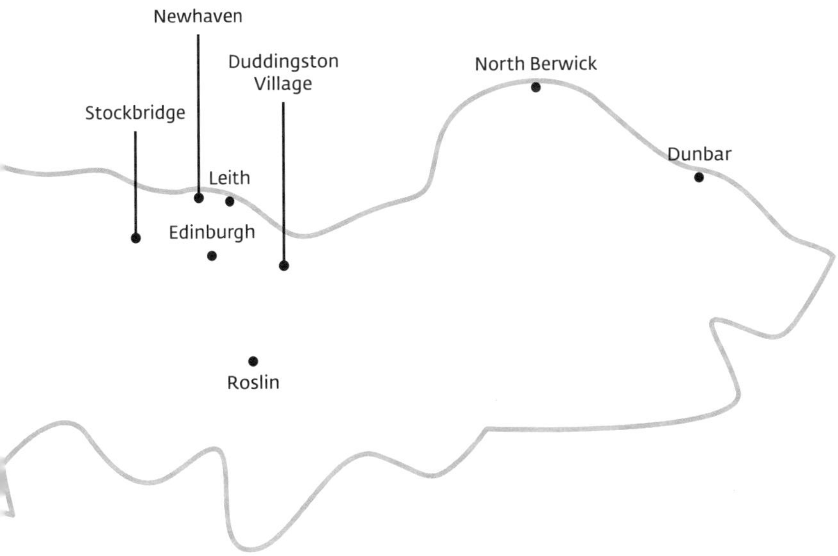
Newhaven
Duddingston Village
North Berwick
Stockbridge
Dunbar
Leith
Edinburgh
Roslin

3 SCOTTISH BORDERS

4 GLASGOW & SOUTH

5 ARGYLL & BUTE

6 LOCH LOMOND & TROSSACHS

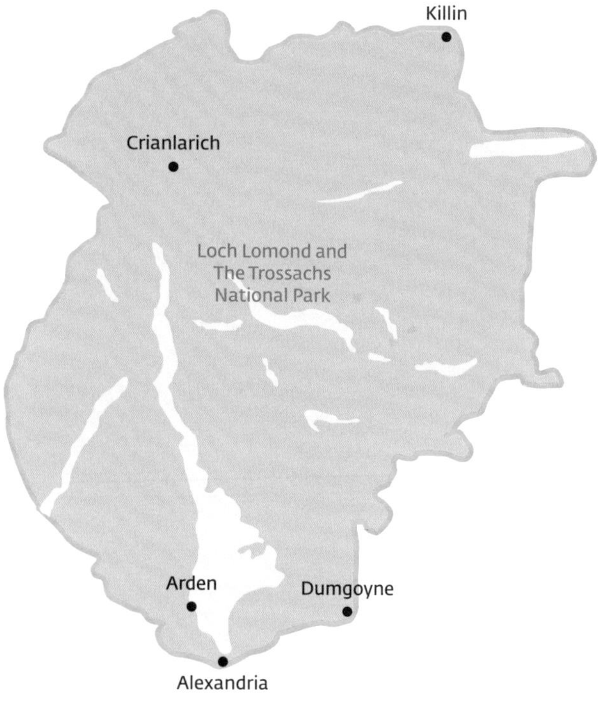

7 HIGHLANDS & ISLANDS

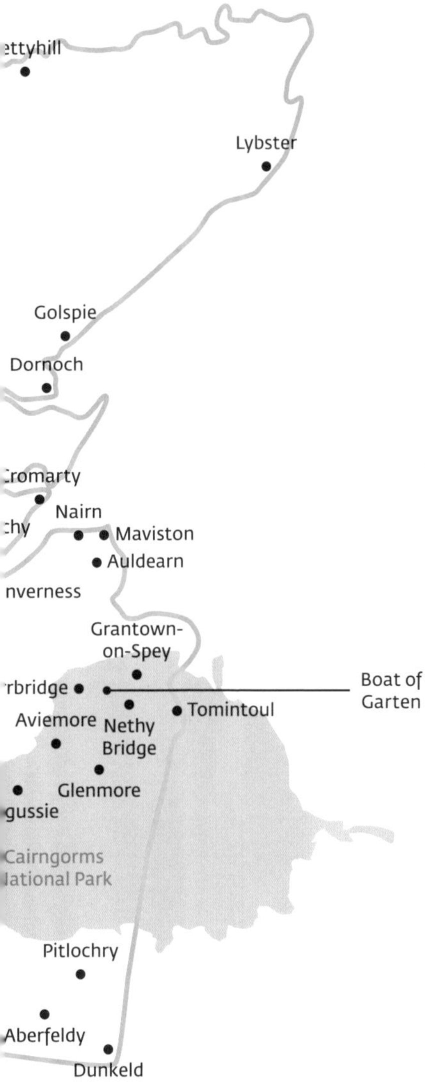
ttyhill
Lybster
Golspie
Dornoch
romarty
Nairn
hy
Maviston
Auldearn
nverness
Grantown-
on-Spey
rbridge
Boat of
Garten
Tomintoul
Aviemore
Nethy
Bridge
Glenmore
gussie
Cairngorms
ational Park
Pitlochry
Aberfeldy
Dunkeld

8 NORTH

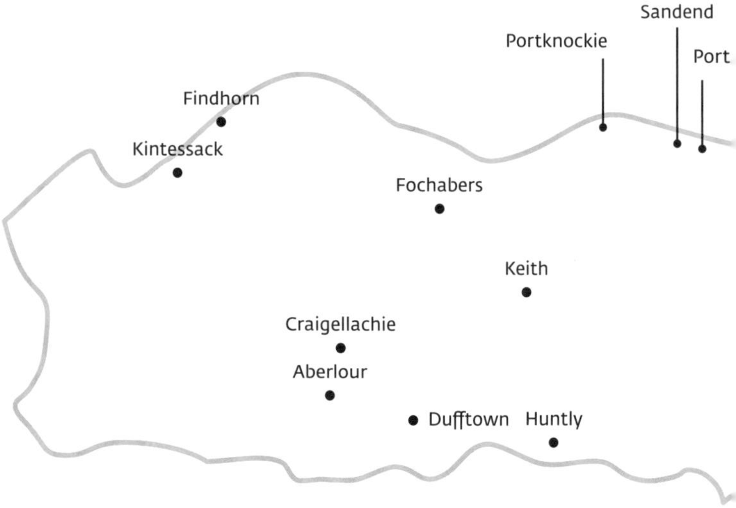
Sandend
Portknockie
Port
Findhorn
Kintessack
Fochabers
Keith
Craigellachie
Aberlour
Dufftown
Huntly

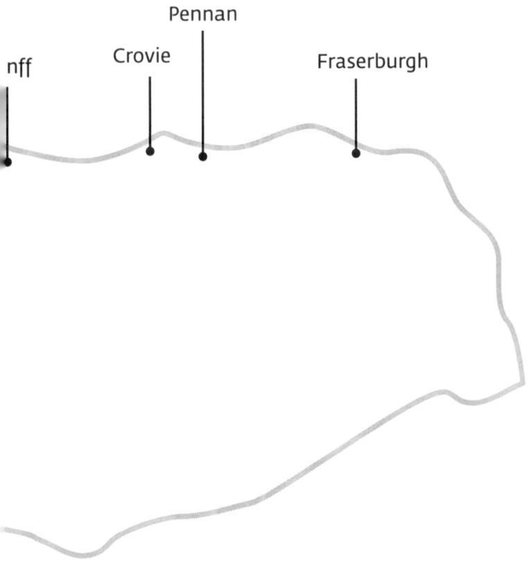

HUNTLY

149 Orb's Bookshop

KEITH

89 Strathisla Distillery

KINTESSACK

102 Culbin Forest

PORTKNOCKIE

122 Bow Fiddle Rock

PORTSOY

35 The Salmon Bothy

235 Portsoy Coffee Shop & Bistro

9 NORTH EAST

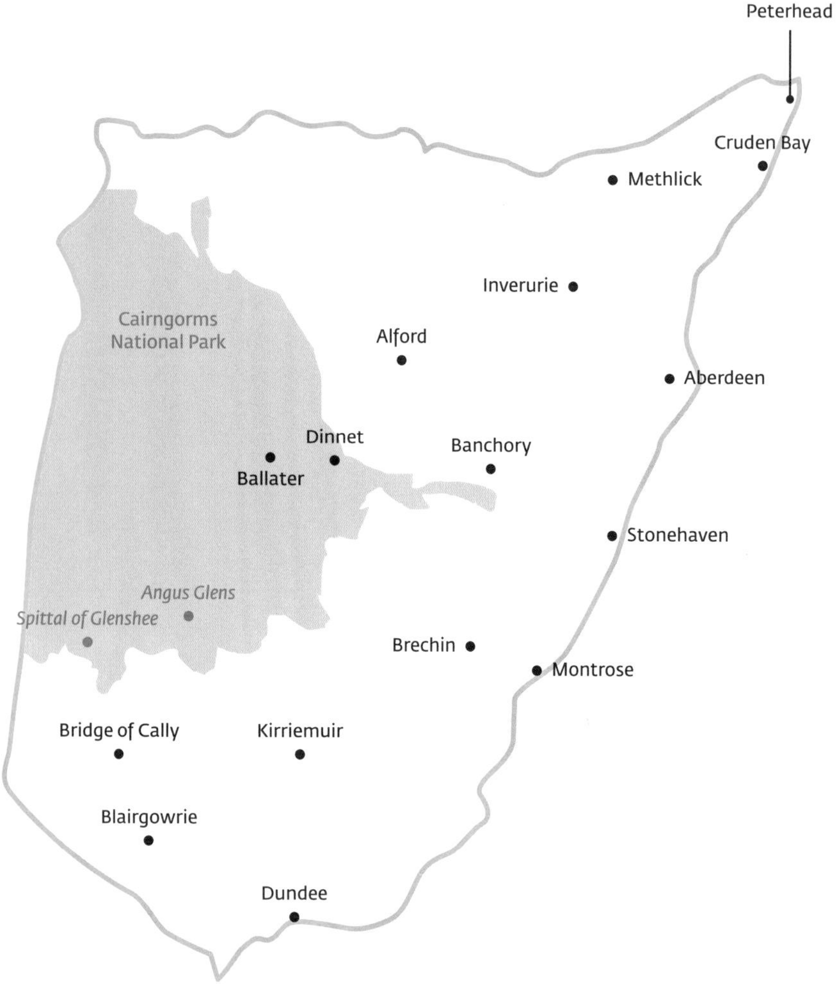

Peterhead
Cruden Bay
Methlick
Inverurie
Alford
Aberdeen
Cairngorms
National Park
Dinnet
Banchory
Ballater
Stonehaven
Angus Glens
Spittal of Glenshee
Brechin
Montrose
Bridge of Cally
Kirriemuir
Blairgowrie
Dundee

THE V&A DUNDEE

ART *and* CULTURE A

Expressive VENUES

1 **SUMMERHALL**
1 Summerhall
Edinburgh
EH9 1PL
+44 (0)131 560 1580
summerhall.co.uk

'Open Minds Open Doors.' Summerhall's slogan perfectly sums up this beautiful multi-arts space. Situated on the corner of the Meadows in an old veterinary school, this place has something for everyone. Workshops, club nights, visual arts, performing arts and everything in between, just take your pick! In August, during the Edinburgh Festival Fringe, Summerhall is a must-visit venue and can comfortably claim to be one of the best arts venues in the world. And definitely one of Scotland's great cultural hubs. There is also a cafe and shop. For their bar and gin distillery see chapter Drinks (Royal Dick).

2 **DCA – DUNDEE CONTEMPORARY ARTS**
152 Nethergate
Dundee
DD1 4DY
North East
+44 (0)1382 432 444
dca.org.uk

DCA is an award-winning contemporary arts centre with limitless options to enjoy. There are two cinema screens, two substantial gallery spaces, a print studio, a shop and a cafe bar. That's not to mention the busy calendar of events, workshops, and classes aimed to educate, empower and inspire. The Taster Sessions are a lot of fun. The Jute Café Bar offers a great menu or a place to grab a drink before or after a movie. The shop is stocked with lots of interesting and unusual gifts, which are a great way to remember your time here.

1 SUMMERHALL

3 **BARROWLAND BALLROOM**

244 Gallowgate
Glasgow
G4 0TT
+44 (0)141 552 4601
barrowland-ballroom.co.uk

The Barrowlands aka 'the Barras' is a Glasgow institution. Opened in 1934, its famous neon signs give you a warm fuzzy feeling and pulls you in like midges to the light. Inside you're met with the famous Glaswegian welcome and a lively crowd. The main hall is famous for its excellent acoustics (essential for the unamplified orchestras it was originally created for) and its sprung dance floor, guaranteed to put a smile on your face! David Bowie, Oasis, U2, and Metallica are just a few of the artists to have played here. However they host everything from hip-hop to electronic nights. Don't expect much from the bar and let yourself be charmed by its faded glamour, you won't regret it.

4 **FINDHORN FOUNDATION**

AT: THE PARK
Findhorn, Forres
IV36 3TZ
North
+44 (0)1309 690 806
findhorn.org

The Findhorn Foundation is a spiritual ecovillage just a stone's throw away from Findhorn village. Started in 1963 from just a caravan, the community is now one of the leading pioneers in sustainable thinking and living, both in Scotland and internationally. Education is at the heart of the foundation, there are workshops and learning opportunities to suit the freest of thinkers and experimenters around. The Great Hall is where many of these events take place, and it's a magical building with its rounded lines and stained glass.

5 HOUSE FOR AN ART LOVER

AT: BELLAHOUSTON PARK

10 Dumbreck Road
Glasgow
G41 5BW
+44 (0)141 483 1600
housefor anartlover.co.uk

The plans for the 'House for an Art Lover' were originally submitted to a German magazine in 1901 by Glasgow's most lamented architect Charles Rennie Mackintosh. They were entered for a competition from which he was later disqualified on the grounds of technical breach of the rules. His plans where eventually realised 80 years later in an effort led by Professor Andy MacMillan, former Head of Architecture at Mackintosh's world-famous Glasgow School of Art, now unfortunately in a state of disrepair. The story, gardens, cafe and studio pavilion make this a great place to spend an afternoon.

4 FINDHORN FOUNDATION

6 **CAOL RUADH SCULPTURE PARK**
Colintraive
PA22 3AR
Argyll & Bute
+44 (0)1700 841 357
scottishsculpturepark.com

Caol Ruadh Sculpture Park is a unique outdoor gallery showcasing some very interesting and beautiful pieces of sculpture. Opened in 2012 the park aims to display and promote the best of Scottish sculptors, and it achieves that in such a wonderful setting. Only open in the summer months, check if it's open before you travel.

7 **THE GREAT POLISH MAP OF SCOTLAND**
AT: BARONY CASTLE HOTEL
Old Manse Road
Eddleston
EH45 8QW
Scottish Borders
mapascotland.org
baronycastle.com

The Great Polish Map of Scotland was nearly lost until it was rediscovered in the late 1990s and fully restored in 2017. Built by a Polish sergeant, who was stationed in Galashiels and married a Scottish nurse after getting injured in 1942, it is now believed to be the largest terrain relief model in the world. The outdoor concrete map was built to scale 1:10.000 and is a fascinating depiction of Scotland, and is categorised as a B listed building, giving it special recognition and protection.

8 GARDEN OF COSMIC SPECULATION

Dumfries
DG2 0RW
South
gardenofcosmic speculation.com

The Garden of Cosmic Speculation is a private garden that opens up to the public only once a year, usually around the first May bank holiday. You can buy tickets from Scotland's Gardens Scheme, which raises money for charities and in this case the Maggie's Cancer Centres, which the curator co-founded. Charles Jencks created this landscape phenomenon through the inspiration of space and time. Its many twists and turns are calculated with mathematics and equal to a mesmerising experience. Check the website for opening times and tickets.

Grand **GALLERIES**

9 **SCOTTISH NATIONAL GALLERY OF MODERN ART**
75 Belford Road
Edinburgh
EH4 3DR
+44 (0)131 624 6200
nationalgalleries.org

This stunning gallery is split over two buildings. Modern One and Modern Two. Modern One, formally John Watson's School for fatherless children, displays an impressive sculpture park and mesmerising landscape architecture designed by Charles Jencks outside the 1825 neoclassical building. Modern Two was originally built as an orphanage hospital in 1833. Combined they house Scotland's outstanding collection of modern and contemporary art. There is something for everyone to take away, irrespective of your art preference. And spaces have been beautiful curated for maximum effect.

10 **SCOTTISH NATIONAL PORTRAIT GALLERY**
1 Queen St
Edinburgh
EH2 1JD
+44 (0)131 624 6200
nationalgalleries.org

The Scottish National Portrait Gallery is truly one of a kind. Built as a shrine for Scotland's heroes it is one of the most impressive buildings in the country, and the first dedicated portrait gallery in the world. Opened to the public in 1889, the building welcomes you under the watchful sculpted eye of Scottish legends Robert the Bruce and William Wallace. You are then met with a stunning visual interpretation of Scottish history on the main hall pageant frieze. Here you can fully appreciate with such chronological beauty what this small nation has brought the world. A proud moment of reflection for some. A unique experience not to be missed, go get inspired. Free admission with some paid exhibitions. The BP Portrait Awards are a must see.

11 GOMA

Royal Exchange Square
Glasgow
G1 3AH
+44 (0)141 287 3050
glasgowlife.org.uk

The Gallery of Modern Art is right at the heart of Glasgow. The neoclassical building was built in 1778 and originally belonged to William Cunninghame, a rich merchant and tobacco lord. The museum does not dance around or hide the fact that its beginnings were certainly tied to slavery, and today the museum is committed to addressing contemporary social issues through its exhibitions. The space is grand and provokes thought and questioning about what is happening in the world around us. What part we play, and where we want to go. Free admission with cafe.

11 GOMA

12 **ST MUNGO MUSEUM OF RELIGIOUS LIFE AND ART**

2 Castle St
Glasgow
G4 0RH
+44 (0)141 276 1625
glasgowlife.org.uk

Let's be honest, Glasgow has a pretty convoluted history with religion. It hasn't always been pretty, but this space only promotes education and acceptance to both the most devout and most sceptic amongst us. Named after the patron saint of Glasgow, the museum shows art and artefacts from the world's largest religions. There is a floor dedicated to Scotland, which illustrates how religion has influenced and dictated opinion for over 5000 years. The zen garden at the back was the first in Britain and the overlooking Glasgow cathedral the oldest building in Scotland.

13 **PETERHEAD PRISON MUSEUM**

South Road
Peterhead
AB42 2YY
North East
+44 (0)1779 581 060
peterhead prisonmuseum.com

Peterhead Prison, also known as Scotland's Alcatraz, was made notorious by the 1987 riots, when prisoners took control of D hall and took two guards hostage. The siege rampaged for 5 days until home secretary Douglas Hurd decided to send in the SAS (British Special Forces) to take back control. Jackie Stuart, who is now in his late 80s, was one of the guards taken captive and works now at the museum as a guide. The tour is interesting and provides a thought-provoking insight into Scotland's only convict prison.

14 THE V&A DUNDEE

1 Riverside Esplanade
Dundee
DD1 4EZ
North East
+44 (0)1382 411 611
vam.ac.uk/dundee

This truly unique and outstanding building makes quite the impression on the Dundee skyline. Designed by Japanese architect Kengo Kuma, its form is said to be inspired by the cliffs of the North East and is quite the structure to ponder over. It's the first ever museum in Scotland dedicated to design and showcases some of the most influential and inspiring collections of international and Scottish design, both physically and virtually and certainly is a bold statement to begin with. Ten years in the making, it's a grand addition to the UNESCO city of design.

14 THE V&A DUNDEE

15 NATIONAL MUSEUM OF SCOTLAND

15 NATIONAL MUSEUM OF SCOTLAND

Chambers St
Edinburgh
EH1 1JF
+44 (0)300 123 6789
nms.ac.uk

Right in the centre of Edinburgh lies the National Museum of Scotland. Formed in 2006 by merging together the Museum of Scotland and the Royal Museum, which lied adjacent. The two buildings now come together to form an outstanding experience. The grand central hall draws in an abundance of light that highlights the grandness of the cast iron construction, dating back to 1866. The exhibitions consist of ancient Egypt, technology, the natural world to name but a few. However the most important and some of the most impressive pieces can be found in the Scottish History and Archaeology display. Here you can find artefacts from the earliest cultures. Learn about Scotland's history, how we were governed, what we have contributed, and take a moment to reflect on where we want to go as a nation. Both intrinsically and internationally. The Museum Late Nights during the Edinburgh Festival Fringe are not to be missed, and are an incredible way to spend your evening. Give yourself time to work around this magnificent building.

16 RIVERSIDE MUSEUM

Pointhouse Place
Glasgow
G3 8RS
+44 (0)141 287 2720
glasgowlife.org.uk

The Riverside museum is a fascinating structure that stands out in the skyline and was designed by the late Zaha Hadid. It houses the Glasgow Transport Museum. The collection has every mode of transport you can think of: from old buses and locomotives to prams, trams and bicycles. Fun and interactive displays, that make learning about our industrial past engaging. Great day out.

ROYAL BOTANIC GARDEN EDINBURGH

DISCOVER

Horticultural

GREEN HEAVENS

17 **DR NEIL'S GARDEN**
Old Church Lane
Duddingston Village
EH15 3PX
Edinburgh
+44 (0)7849 187 995
drneilsgarden.co.uk

Dr Neil's Garden is somewhat of a hidden sanctuary where Arthur's Seat meets Duddingston Loch. It is a great place to come and get fresh air or reflect on days past. The Garden was started by couple Nancy and Andrew Neil, who both worked as GPs at the time. They used to encourage their patients to aid in the creation of the space, so they could benefit from being active and adopt healthier lifestyles. Nancy and Andrew both passed away in 2005 and their legacy lives on throughout the grounds, and specifically in the physical garden. Thomson's Tower is another quirky addition to the gardens, built in 1825 for the Duddingston Curling Society to store its stones. The lower chamber is now a curling museum and tells an interesting story on how one club has influenced the way the game is played today. Today there are various ways to enjoy the garden through art, educational events and healthy activity. The Garden Room Cafe is open in the summer.

18 ROYAL BOTANIC GARDEN EDINBURGH

Arboretum Place
Edinburgh
EH3 5NZ
+44 (0)131 248 2909
rbge.org.uk

The 'Botanics' in Edinburgh is a horticultural haven set in 70 acres and only a mile from the city centre. On a sunny day it's a fantastic place to stroll, chill out and enjoy the vast living collections, which are 350 years old. Throughout the garden there are 10 different glass houses, with the highlight being a stunning Victorian Temperate Palm House, which is the largest of its kind in Britain and constructed in 1858. Amongst the 100.000 exotic plants, Chinese gardens and Amazonian lily pads, the Scottish Heath Garden and the native plants are the most humble, homely (for some) and not to be overlooked. Go and enjoy one of the most stunning botanical gardens in the world.

18 ROYAL BOTANIC GARDEN EDINBURGH

19 THE LADY LINDA MCCARTNEY MEMORIAL GARDEN

Hall St
Campbeltown
PA28 6AD
Argyll & Bute
lindasgarden.co.uk

If you are taking a stroll 'down the front' in Campbeltown, take a mini detour to Linda's Garden. The garden was set up in memory of Paul McCartney's late wife, who was very fond of Argyll – her ashes are scattered here. Paul still owns a farm down this way and wrote the famous 1970s hit, *Mull of Kintyre*, here. It's in a peaceful setting behind the library and a bronze statue of Linda holding a lamb takes centre stage.

Amazing URBAN VIEWS

20 **CALTON HILL**
Regent Road
Edinburgh
EH1 3DG

Calton Hill offers up some of the best panoramic views of the city of Edinburgh and beyond to the Firth of Forth. Get up early and beat the tourists to the top and watch the sunrise hit Arthur's Seat, you won't regret it. The way the city catches the morning sun on a clear day is remarkable. Once you're up there, you can find some of the city's most popular landmarks, such as the unfinished National Monument, the Nelson Monument and the City Observatory. If you don't fancy the early start, grab yourself a quiet corner away from the selfie sticks as it's a great place to grab a beer and bask in the sun.

21 **DUNDEE LAW**
Law Road
Dundee
DD3 6LD
North East

Once an Iron Age hill fort, this 175-metre hill provides epic views over the city, Fife and Perthshire on a clear day. Walk to the top, where a war memorial stands prominent to get the best snaps, and take in this iconic Dundee landmark.

20 **CALTON HILL**

COASTAL *discoveries*

22 CRUCIFIXION CAVE / DAVAAR ISLAND

Campbeltown
PA28 6RE
Argyll & Bute

Davaar Island is a tidal island that sits at the mouth of Campbeltown Loch and is famous for its caves and lighthouse. One particular cave stands out however, as there is a famous painting of the crucifixion that was discovered by a fisherman in 1887. It was thought to have been a sign from God, however it was actually created by local artist Archibald MacKinnon, who had a vision in a dream to do it. It was touched up a couple of times by Archibald, but was defaced in 2006 and the face was painted over with Che Guevara's. It has since been successfully restored. Please check tidal times before crossing (online or at the pier). You are safe to walk 3 hours each way during low tide.

23 FINGAL'S CAVE / STAFFA

1 Top of the Pier
Achavaich,
Isle of Iona
PA76 6SW
Argyll & Bute
nts.org.uk

Staffa is a mesmerising little piece of uninhabited land off the west coast of Scotland in the Inner Hebrides. The hexagon shaped columns rise out of the sea, and were formed millions of years earlier by a volcanic eruption. One of the most fascinating natural formations on Staffa is Fingal's Cave, a 22-metre-tall and 82-metre-wide opening that is perfectly formed. In Gaelic it's known as *Uamh-Binn* or 'cave of the melody', due to its famous acoustics created by the waves splashing against the rocks, creating a unique melody. To get there you will have to take a boat tour. Staffa Tours are recommended and you can depart from Iona, Oban or Mull.

24 CRAMOND ISLAND

Edinburgh
EH4 6NU
queensferry
lifeboat.co.uk

Cramond Island is a uninhabited island that is exciting to explore at low tide. The walkway extends 1,2 kilometre from the village of Cramond and leads to intriguing abandoned wartime lookouts and farm buildings. The walk along the Cramond coastline and out to the island is a great way to kill a few hours, and popular with joggers and dog walkers. Make sure you check and double check the timings of the tides and give yourself plenty of time to return. The tide comes in faster than you think, and you don't want to get stuck!

24 CRAMOND ISLAND

25 WATER OF LEITH

Edinburgh

The Water of Leith starts in the outskirts at Balerno in the Pentland Hills and finishes when it reaches the Firth of Forth at Leith. You can follow the river by walking its footpath. It is at its most picturesque when it reaches the Dean Village to Stockbridge then to Leith. Enjoy a stroll...

26 KEIL'S CAVE AND ST COLUMBA'S STEPS

Southend, Campbeltown PA28 6RW Argyll & Bute

After you have stopped at Muneroy Tearoom, this is an excellent way to walk off the meringues. Park at the Keil Point car park, not far from St Columba's Chapel and walk back to the iron gate. From there you can navigate to either the footsteps or the caves. The caves have different names such as the Pipers Cave, Great Cave and Hermit's Retreat. They have had various forms of occupancy over the past centuries, and Roman pottery has been found here. The 1881 census reported that two families lived here by the names of McFee and McCallum. Piper's Cave is also believed to be haunted, due to the disappearance of a piper whilst passing on his way home. You can seemingly still hear his ghost play his pipes. St Columba's Steps are a pair of footprints carved into the rock. One of them is ancient and the other was carved by a local stone mason in 1856. Marking footsteps in stones is usually related with crowning ceremonies, so it's unclear why they exist here. However they are still an interesting symbol to mark Saint Columba – the man who brought Christianity to Scotland – landing here.

27 WHALIGOE STEPS

Lybster
KW2 6AB
Highlands & Islands

Step down the Whaligoe Steps to go back in time. These steps where created in 1786 and descend from a steep cliff edge, they lead you to what was one of Scotland's most inaccessible harbours, sheltered by the 76-metre cliffs towering overhead. Thomas Telford, the famous Scottish architect and stonemason, described it as a 'dreadful place' for a harbour, however Captain David Brodie wasn't discouraged and paid a local stonemason £8 to cut 330 steps down, which paid off as by 1814 there were around 14 herring boats operating here. You can still see the ruins of the salt house below, where women would gut and prepare the fish and store them in salted barrels. There was a cooperage at the top of the cliffs and women would haul the barrels down, along with fresh catches up the steps to be sold at Wick 11 kilometres away. They were hard as nails back in those days! Today it's just a spectacular vista laced with history and a bit of a challenge navigating the steps down and up. However you can reward yourself with a cake at the fantastic cafe up the top. The Whaligoe Steps are NOT signposted, so you're better off following signs for the Cairn o'Get, where the steps are not far.

28 CLOOTIE WELL

A832
Munlochy
IV8 8AD
Highlands & Islands

Clootie Well is believed to date back to pre-Christian times around 620 AD. It served as a holy well where pagan rituals were carried out and offerings were given to the local spirits and gods. The well is believed to have healing powers. The word *cloot* in Scots means a cloth or rag. Pilgrims would (and still do) tie them to the trees. Traditionally the *cloot* would have been in contact with the person who has the ailment and – after a ritual and prayer – tied to a tree to decompose. As the rag fades away, so does the illness. However, the problem in recent times is that visitors are tying synthetic rags to the trees, which do not break down. So if you wish to partake in this ancient ritual, please do so respectfully using biodegradable natural fabrics. After the Reformation of 1560 a law was passed making pilgrimages to holy wells illegal, suppressing and rejecting the traditional Celtic norms of the Scottish Church, making this an even more significant, superstitious and eerie visit to this small well.

28 CLOOTIE WELL

30 WALK TO THE DEVIL'S PULPIT / FINNICH GLEN

29 BELHAVEN BRIDGE

20 Shore Road
Dunbar
EH42 1NX
Lothians

Belhaven Bridge or the 'bridge to nowhere' seems the oddest thing at high tide. The bridge looks stranded with no purpose whatsoever as the water engulfs the bases. However at low tide, the bridge serves to allow access to the sandy beach on the other side of a small outflow stream. The bridge has allowed many an interesting Instagram picture for professional and amateur photographers alike.

30 THE DEVIL'S PULPIT / FINNICH GLEN

A809
Dumgoyne
G63 9QL
Loch Lomond & Trossachs

Finnich Glen or the Devil's Pulpit is steeped in mysterious folklore. It's named after a protruding bulbous type rock that you can spot at low waters and looks like a pulpit. It's here where the devil was said to have stood and addressed his worshippers and where black magic druids held secret meetings, out of the surveillance of prosecuting eyes. The river runs red and is said to reflect the blood of the victims, however it's the red sandstone of the gorge that gives it this colour and the green moss adds to the eerie feel. Given its dark history, this is a beautiful place to explore within the 21-metre-high walls. Please note that the Devil's Pulpit is difficult to access and should be avoided after heavy rainfall. It's steep, slippery and dangerous when the water is high. So correct footwear and care is needed. Parking can also be an issue, as there are not many spaces. So please apply common sense.

31 ADVOCATE'S CLOSE

Royal Mile
Edinburgh
EH1 1ND

Once you've stomped up and down the Royal Mile and want to get out the way of tourists, peel off down Advocate's Close, a steep and narrow lane that is believed to date back to 1544. The dark shadows remind you of Edinburgh's haunting past. You exit on Cockburn Street if coming from the Royal Mile, and it gives you excellent views over to Princes Street, Scott Monument and the Old Town.

31 ADVOCATE'S CLOSE

Impressive MANORS

32 **MOUNT STUART HOUSE**

Isle of Bute
PA20 9LR
Argyll & Bute
+44 (0)1700 503877
mountstuart.com

This monumental 19th-century Gothic revival mansion has to be seen to be believed. Originally built in 1719, and again in 1877, by the 3rd Marquess of Bute after a fire, it was renowned as one of the most technologically advanced houses of its era. Extravagance and imagination are what you'll find here, with a stunning white marble chapel, astrology-inspired ceilings and a grand 300-acre garden that is a botanical beauty and a pleasure to be in. Mount Stuart has been committed to ensuring the public can access and enjoy the house, grounds, art collections and archives for quite some time now. The visual arts and exhibitions are an exciting addition and should not be missed. The cafe Bute Kitchen has a great selection of locally sourced food, and you can even pre-book a luxury picnic ahead to enjoy in the grounds. Worth paying the money for the tour, and a great day out in one of Scotland's most impressive buildings.

33 HADDO HOUSE

Methlick
AB41 7EQ
North East
+44 (0)1651 851 440
nts.org.uk

Take a stroll around the large and beautiful gardens of Haddo House. This stately home was in the same family for over 400 years and is now owned and managed by the National Trust for Scotland. There is a terrace garden, a country park, an adventure playground and a cafe. Giving you lots of options to pick from. You can also tour the house, which takes around 70 minutes and lets you get more personal with this grand home.

34 DUFF HOUSE

34 DUFF HOUSE

Banff
AB45 3SX
North
+44 (0)1261 818 181
historic environment.scot

This large Georgian mansion has a complicated history. Construction began in 1735 for William Duff, a successful businessman and sharp politician. Duff House was something of a vanity project and Scottish architect William Adam was chosen to execute the vision of wealth. However works stopped in 1741 due to diminishing funds, and a five-year court battle proceeded, which favoured Adam, except he died before he received the debit owed to him. After all that, Duff then decided not to sleep one night in the mansion, because he was so disappointed, and work was left to the heirs to complete. At the start of the 20th century the Duff family married into the royal family and the house was gifted and adopted for many uses including a hotel, a sanatorium and a prisoner-of-war camp. In 1940 the house was damaged during a bombing raid by the German Luftwaffe. Duff House was reopened to the public in 1995 and is a country house gallery and displays a grand collection of art from the National Galleries of Scotland. An interesting stop-off if you are near the pretty coastal towns of Banff and Macduff.

Eclectic HISTORY

35 **THE SALMON BOTHY**
Links Road
Portsoy
AB45 2SS
North
+44 (0)1261 842 951
salmonbothy.org

The Salmon Bothy is a former working salmon house, and has now been restored into a museum and community space. Salmon farming is an important part of this coastline's history, and the museum exists to show artefacts from this time and celebrate the rich culture that went with this industry. Using the Bothy as a base for family research is also recommended and a qualified genealogist is available by appointment. There is also a catalogue of ancestor charts to help you with your search. Great little venue, that's worth a pop-in visit if you're in the area.

36 **THE GOVAN STONES**
AT: GOVAN OLD PARISH CHURCH
866 Govan Road
Glasgow
G51 3UU
+44 (0)141 440 2466
thegovanstones.org.uk

The Govan stones are a series of 9th to 11th-century carved stones displayed in the beautiful Govan Old Parish Church. They are an outstanding collection which reflects the power struggles that went on in the Kingdom of Strathclyde. The five hogback gravestones are incredible and the intricately carved Govan sarcophagus is the only one of its kind in the UK from pre-Norman times. These 31 stones are a precious and fascinating depiction of Scotland's complicated history. Entry is free, but donations are most welcome.

37 CULLODEN HILL

AT: CULLODEN VISITOR CENTRE

Culloden Moor
Inverness
IV2 5EU
Highlands & Islands
+44 (0)1463 796 090
nts.org.uk/visit/places/culloden

Culloden is far from a hidden secret, but it's one of Scotland's most significant locations in regards to history and culture. Scotland would no doubt look wildly different today if the '45 Rebellion were to have won the Battle of Culloden on the 16th of April 1746. Certainly, the face of the Highlands was changed forever. It was said that nothing grew properly on the battlefield for years. But now you can spot foxgloves, rowans, willow and earth nut that would have been essential use for medicinal purposes in the 18th century. Great visitor centre dedicated to a fascinating time in Scottish history. Tours strongly recommended and a great cafe to grab a coffee.

37 CULLODEN HILL

NEW SLAINS CASTLE

BUILDINGS

RELIGIOUS *grounds*

38 MELROSE ABBEY

Abbey St
Melrose
TD6 9LG
Scottish Borders
+44 (0)1896 822 562
historic environment.scot

Famously the burial place of King Robert the Bruce's lead-encased heart, Melrose Abbey is an intriguing and captivating ruin, which has played a pivotal role in Scotland's history. Founded in 1136 by Cistercian monks at the request of King David the First of Scotland, the abbey was built to display power, given its proximity to the English border. Only a very small proportion of the original abbey exists, due to scathing attacks from English kings over the years. One of the most destructive being Richard II's attack in 1385. These brutal attacks have led to different architectural styles being applied through rebuilding efforts throughout the hundreds of years. The sculptures that adorn the exterior are a bagpipe-playing pig, lute-playing angels and cooks with ladles. Keep an eye out when studying the spectacular medieval architecture. You can also experience Scotland's largest collection of medieval artefacts at the Commendator's House Museum that is situated at the north end of the site. Step back in time at one of Scotland's grandest historical buildings.

39 KAGYU SAMYE LING MONASTERY

Langholm,
Dumfries
DG13 0QL
South
+44 (0)1387 373 232
samyeling.org

It's not often when exploring the Scottish countryside that you will come across a Buddhist monastery. Founded in 1967, Kagyu Samye Ling is the first Tibetan Buddhist centre developed in the West. The temples, stupas and prayer wheels feel authentic as if you have been transported to far flung places such as Nepal or Tibet. The tearoom is traditional and a nice place to sit and chill, especially once you have slowed down and appreciated the Buddhist way of life here. Courses are regularly held for a variety of topics including yoga, meditation, tai chi and are increasingly popular, especially with the 'mindfulness movement'. A great place to visit, especially if you are curious about the Buddhist world.

39 KAGYU SAMYE LING MONASTERY

40 JEDBURGH ABBEY

4 Abbey Bridge End
Jedburgh
TD8 6JQ
Scottish Borders
+44 (0)1835 863 925
historic environment.scot

Jedburgh is another impressive abbey established in the 1100s in the Scottish Borders by David I. It took over 70 years to build, and like Melrose, incorporates different eras of architecture from Romanesque to Gothic, and shifted from priory to abbey within this time. The site at Jedburgh had been of religious importance 300 years prior and no buildings from this time remain. However architectural finds including crosses and a sarcophagus dating back to the 700s are on display in the visitor centre, along with a beard comb carved from walrus ivory dating back to the 1110s. Elevated views from the walkways give you an interesting perspective on the cloisters and the rest of the Abbey. A truly stunning ruin, with a story to match.

41 MAGDALEN CHAPEL

41 Cowgate
Edinburgh
EH1 1JR
+44 (0)131 220 1450
scottishreformation society.org

This small chapel in the heart of Edinburgh was built around 1541 by Michael MacQueen and his wife Janet Rynd for the Incorporation of Hammermen (those who work with metal and hammer). The medieval stained glass is the only glass to have survived the Scottish Reformation in its original place. Owned by the Hammermen until 1858, it now belongs to the Scottish Reformation Society. The Cowgate in Edinburgh is a haunt for night-time revellers, and many people overlook this chapel and walk past, unaware of its existence. Open Monday to Friday from 10 am to 4 pm.

42 ROSSLYN CHAPEL

Chapel Loan
Roslin
EH25 9PU
Lothians
+44 (0)131 440 2159
rosslynchapel.com

Situated in the village of Roslin just a couple of kilometres south of Edinburgh, Rosslyn Chapel was founded in 1446 and is full of mystery and various conspiracy theories, with some people believing that this is the resting place of the holy grail. Inside you'll discover some of the world's most enigmatic carvings every angle you look, that have been studied carefully over the years to reveal cryptic puzzles and even hidden music. Some of the most famous carvings are of maize, originating from North America, which questions if Columbus founded America in 1492 after all. Building of the chapel was begun by William St Clair, the last prince of Orkney, and has been worked on ever since. With attention to detail and stunning stone masonry that tells enchanting stories, this building is one of the most special in Scotland.

42 ROSSLYN CHAPEL

GRAND *buildings*

43 NATIONAL ARCHIVES OF SCOTLAND – GENERAL REGISTER HOUSE

2 Princes St
Edinburgh
EH1 3YY
nrscotland.gov.uk/research/learning/exhibitions

General Register House sits prominently on the east side on Princes Street and is the oldest custom-built archive building in the world. If you're tracing your ancestry, then your search to your past will probably lead you here. Birth, death, immigration, marriage and slave records are just some of the documentation held here. Construction began in 1752, and was funded by the budget of £12.000 taken from forfeited Jacobite fortune. However money ran out and construction was suspended in 1779. For six years the building laid empty, said to attract unsavoury characters and described as 'the most magnificent pigeon house in Europe'. The most spectacular room in the building is Robert Adam's dome room: 24 metres high and 15 metres wide, naturally lit by the central oculus and inspired by the Pantheon in Rome. It really is a magnificent room and quite an emotional experience connecting the past to the future. Out back is one of the hidden gems, that even many Edinburgh locals don't know about, the Archivists' Gardens. A courtyard planted with 57 different species representing birth, death, marriage, folklore and heraldry. An outstanding building connecting the dots to our internal curiosity of belonging.

44 GLASGOW CITY CHAMBERS

82 George St
Glasgow
G2 1DU
+44 (0)141 287 4018
glasgow.gov.uk

Glasgow City Chambers was designed by Scottish architect William Young and was finished in 1888 and widely renowned as respected piece of Victorian civil architecture. The building was inaugurated by Queen Victoria, with the first council meeting being held in October 1889, and currently serves as the council headquarters. The interior is grand, with mosaic ceilings, marble stair cases and a banquet hall – where Nelson Mandela famously received his Freedom of the City. Free tours are the best way to enjoy this impressive building, they leave Monday to Friday at 10.30 am and 2.30 pm. It operates on a first come, first served basis, so arriving 30 minutes prior to the tour leaving is advised.

44 GLASGOW CITY CHAMBERS

45 GLASGOW UNIVERSITY

University Avenue
Glasgow
G12 8QQ
gla.ac.uk

The University of Glasgow was founded in 1451 and is the fourth oldest university in the world. The university's most impressive building is the Gilbert Scott Building, named after its designer who was a leading figure in the Gothic revival movement. After he died, his son oversaw its completion. It is famous for its tower that stands 85 metres tall. The university chapel was built in 1929 as a memorial to students who passed away in the two world wars and is one of the very few churches in Scotland where Protestant and Roman Catholic marriages can be performed. Leading to the Hunterian Museum (which is definitely worth visiting) you'll have to pass the East and West Quadrangles and under the cloisters. One of the most picturesque areas of the university with the grand high archways. Book a tour to fully appreciate the importance and beauty of this institution.

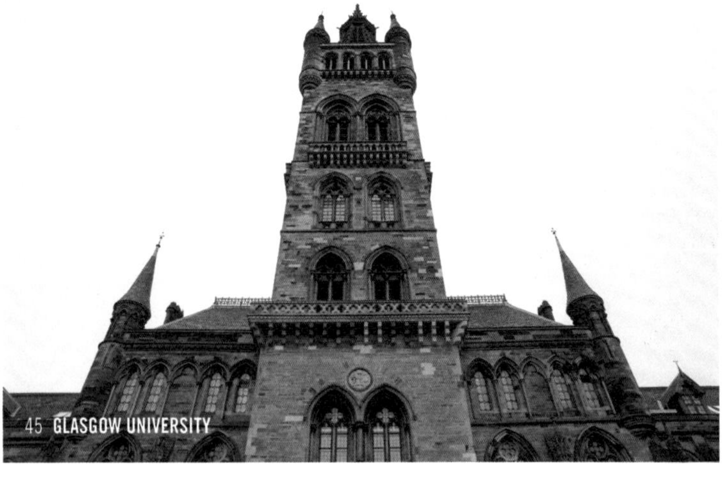
45 GLASGOW UNIVERSITY

46 THE DUNMORE PINEAPPLE

AT: DUNMORE PARK
Near Airth
Falkirk
FK2 8LU
Lothians
+44 (0)1314 580 200
nts.org.uk

The Dunmore Pineapple is a truly fascinating and entertaining building. The lower half of the hothouse was built in 1761 to grow unusual fruits and vegetables. The top pineapple half was said to be built after 1777 when the 4th Earl of Dunmore returned from Virginia, USA after being the last colonial governor and it's believed to be a present for his wife, Charlotte. Pineapples and sugar were a delicacy across Europe, a sign of status, wealth and power, so you can see why building one 14 metres high was priority for some! Great walks around the gardens, and a bizarre but beautiful building to enjoy.

46 **THE DUNMORE PINEAPPLE**

47 **ROYAL OBSERVATORY EDINBURGH**

Blackford Hill
Edinburgh
EH9 3HJ
+44 (0)131 668 8404
www.roe.ac.uk

The ROE is still in use today carrying out astronomical research and university teaching. The original site was on Calton Hill (now called the City Observatory) before moving to its current location on Blackford Hill. The two copper rotating domes stand out with their teal blue oxidised colour. Inside the latest and cutting-edge technology is used to study the night sky. Frequently hosting public events in the evenings, which are a very interesting way to pass the time and learn more about our universe. The ROE is a busy workplace and drop-in visits can't be accommodated. Pre-booking is essential.

48 **GLASGOW WOMEN'S LIBRARY**

23 Landressy St
Glasgow
G40 1BP
+44 (0)141 550 2267
womenslibary.org.uk

Glasgow Women's Library was founded in 1991 and takes home in a stunning renovated former Carnegie Library built in 1903. It is the only accredited museum in the UK dedicated to women's lives, histories and achievements. There is a lending library full of captivating reads and archive collections, too. There is a full schedule of thought-provoking events, workshops and learning opportunities that are open to all. A great place to come and learn, understand and be inspired.

49 THE LIGHTHOUSE

11 Mitchell Lane
Glasgow
G1 3NU
+44 (0)141 276 5365
thelighthouse.co.uk

The Lighthouse is Scotland's centre for design and architecture. The building was designed by Charles Rennie Mackintosh and was previously The Glasgow Herald newspaper's offices. It was also Mackintosh's first public commission, which they have commemorated with a permanent exhibition dedicated to him. The highlights of this building have to be the views. There are two viewing points, one outside accessed by the helical staircase and the other on the 6th floor, giving views of Glasgow's wonderful skyline.

49 VIEW FROM THE LIGHTHOUSE

50 **PROVAND'S LORDSHIP**

Castel St
Glasgow
G4 0RB
+44 (0)141 276 1625
glasgowlife.org.uk

The Provand's Lordship is the oldest house in Glasgow and one of the two oldest medieval buildings. Built in 1471 by the Bishop of Glasgow, it now houses a historic medieval museum. Free admission.

50 PROVAND'S LORDSHIP

51 GOVANHILL BATHS

99 Calder St
Glasgow
G42 7RA
+44 (0)141 433 2999
govanhillbaths.com

Govanhill Baths is that last remaining Edwardian public bathhouse in Glasgow. It was opened to the public in 1917, and apart from leisure, an important function of the building was to provide steam laundry facilities to local residents living in tenement buildings, who didn't have such facilities. Officially shut in 2001, the future for this excellent building looked bleak. However, an array of events from art, poetry, and theatre has kept the spirit alive. And steady campaigning from Community group, Govanhill Baths Community Trust could see the building be restored. A great piece of Glasgow history. Govanhill Baths building is now closed to the public for renovation but their services continue in a variety of venues in Govanhill.

HISTORICAL *homes*

52 ELCHO CASTLE

Rhynd, Perth
PH2 8QQ
Central Scotland
+44 (0)1738 639 998
historic environment.scot

Elcho Castle is the place to go if you want to get a real feel of what it was like to live in a fortified mansion in the 16th century. Mostly complete, you can tour around this impressive building and head to the top walkway to gain the best vantage for views across Perthshire.

53 KELLIE CASTLE

Pittenweem
KY10 2RE
Central Scotland
+44 (0)1333 720 271
nts.org.uk

Built in 1360 and abandoned in 1829 after the 10th Earl of Kellie died with no direct heirs, this castle was destined for ruin and by 1860 the great hall was being used as a barn. However, the castle's fate was to change when a family from Edinburgh holidaying in the area came across Kellie and decided to take on the challenge of renovation and secured a 38-year lease. The family was a famous architectural and arts family called the Lorimers, who reinstated the castle to its glory, displaying some of the oldest plaster ceilings in Scotland. The walled garden and woodland walks provide for some lovely fresh air, and the tearoom is a great wee place to rest the legs.

54 SMAILHOLM TOWER

Sandyknowe Farm
Kelso
TD5 7PG
Scottish Borders
+44 (0)1573 460 365
historic environment.scot

Smailholm is a tall skinny tower house that sits alone at the top of a rocky outcrop, surveying the surrounding landscape. It stands at 20 metres tall and has walls two metres thick, that were essential to defence in this constantly contested land near the border. Sir Walter Scott was sent to this place as a sickly young child for the good of his health, where he was looked after by his grandmother and aunt. They used to read him stories about the Borders' countryside and he later described the impact that it had on him and his imagination. He had one last poignant visit here before his death in 1832 and is buried in Dryburgh Abbey not far away.

55 CRAIGIEVAR CASTLE

Alford
AB33 8JF
North East
+44 (0)1339 883 635
nts.org.uk

This seven-storey tower house started in 1576 and finished around 1626 is a picture-perfect fairy-tale castle, and said to be the inspiration for Walt Disney's Cinderella castle. The pink walls stand out against the charming woodland, in which there are great walks to enjoy and take in the peace of the countryside.

56 DUNROBIN CASTLE

Golspie
KW10 6SF
Highlands & Islands
+44 (0)1408 633 177
dunrobincastle.co.uk

Dunrobin Castle has 189 rooms and looks more at home in a fairy-tale book than it does in the Scottish Highlands. It has been home to the Earls and Dukes of Sutherland since the 13th century and has undergone many transformations since. The most distinctive being the 1845 Charles Barry renovation that was very much French château in inspiration. With grand rounded spires and formal gardens. Despite how impressive and luxurious this castle is, it is somewhat controversial. The Sutherlands were responsible for some of the most brutal acts of the Highland Clearances, and the upgrading of the castle is remembered to be made possible by the wealth earned by clearing the Gaelic Highlanders off their land. Whatever your persuasion, it is still an interesting castle to visit and learn from.

56 DUNROBIN CASTLE

ABANDONED *beauties*

57 OLD CASTLE LACHLAN

B800
Barnacarry
PA21 2EP
Argyll & Bute
oldcastlelachlan.com

Old Castle Lachlan is a beautiful little ruin on the banks of Loch Fyne. It serves as head of the MacLachlan clan, who are one of the oldest Scottish Highland clans, and were faithful Jacobite soldiers. The castle came into ruin after the Battle of Culloden in 1746, where their 17th chief was killed. It is said that a government ship sailed up the loch and shelled the castle after the defeat and hasn't been habited since. Today there is great walks around the castle, and it's a great place for a picnic or to stretch out after your epic dinner at Inver.

58 EDZELL CASTLE AND GARDEN

Brechin
DD9 7UE
North East
+44 (0)1356 648 603
historic environment.scot

Edzell Castle is a ruined castle built in the 1500s, which was home to the powerful Lindsay family, who hosted famous guests such as Mary, Queen of Scots. The Lindsays had to sell Edzell in 1715 because of mounting debts and the new owner, Earl of Panmure, lost it because of his role in the Jacobite rising. This castle nobles' residence might be over, but its gardens certainly aren't. The walled garden or 'Pleasance' was built in 1604 and is a marvellous walled garden to visit. In the walls you can spot a series of carved panels that depict the seven cardinal virtues, the liberal arts and the planetary deities. They are unique to Scotland and are said to have links with esoteric traditions and freemasonry.

60 DUNNOTTAR CASTLE

59 NEW SLAINS CASTLE

A975
Cruden Bay
AB42 0NE
North East

Slains Castle is a very impressive ruin that lies just outside Cruden Bay. Constructed in 1597 the castle looms over the cliffs edge, and has a slight eerie feel to it. It's no wonder then why this castle served as serious inspiration for Bram Stoker's famous Dracula. Be careful when exploring the castle and near the cliffs, especially when it's windy, as it's easy to lose footing. Park in the small car park off the A975 or take the slighty longer walk in from Cruden Bay. "Once again...welcome to my house. Come freely. Go safely; and leave something of the happiness you bring." – Bram Stoker, Dracula

60 DUNNOTTAR CASTLE

Stonehaven
AB39 2TL
North East
+44 (0)1569 766 320
dunnottar castle.co.uk

Dunnottar Castle or *Dùn Fhoithear* in Gaelic means 'Fort on the shelving slope' and describes one of the most influential medieval castles in Scotland's history. The heavily fortified ruin stands strong 49 metres above the North Sea and is bursting with history. The oldest Pictish fort to ever be found was discovered just north of the castle, legends like William Wallace have captured it and Mary, Queen of Scots, and James VI have both been visitors here. The views are stunning, looking out across the narrow path to the castle, and the tour is well worth paying for. If you want to walk to the castle from Stonehaven, there is a great cliff top walk. Download the simple map from the Dunnottar website. Not to be missed if you are 'castle bagging'.

61 CASTLE TIORAM

Eilean Tioram
Loch Moidart / River Shiel
Doirlinn
Highlands & Islands
moidart.org.uk

Ruined Castle Tioram sits on a rocky tidal island and stands imposing over Loch Moidart. Its location must have been significant, especially in pre-industrial times when seas, lochs and rivers were the most efficient way to navigate Scotland's rugged west coast. It is also in the middle of a historic trade route out to the western isles. The castle has historically been at the centre of the MacDonalds of Clanranald, who are responsible for a lot of friction between clans of the Highlands and Islands and the monarchy. It was seized by the government in 1692, due to clan chief Allan of Clanranald defaulting to the Jacobites in France, however he recaptured it in 1715 during the Jacobite uprising and burnt it to the ground to stop it falling back into government hands. It's been a ruin ever since. Turn off the A861 for signposted road towards 'Castle Dorlin' as the locals refer to it. Follow the single-track road and park at the car park at the end. From there, walk across the beach to the castle. Bear in mind tidal times. And be careful of falling masonry when exploring, the 13th-century ruin is very unstable.

ROAD TO PLOCKTON

PLACES

Fine places **TO MEET**

62 **THE HIDDEN LANE**
1103 Argyle St
Glasgow
G3 8ND
thehiddenlane glasgow.com

Just off Argyle Street you'll find a cluster of creatives down a lane, hidden from plain sight. The brightly coloured buildings are each stamped with their own individuality and the community of artists, designers, musicians and general creatives work in about 100 studios. Spoilt for choice with a truly unique shopping experience, there are also exhibitions, yoga and music lessons on offer. Go get creative!

63 **ASHTON LANE**
West End
Glasgow
G12 85J

Jam-packed with lively bars and restaurants, the charming cobbled streets and low-hung fairy lights greet you with a warm and friendly vibe. Climb the stairs to the top of Ubiquitous Chip and chill out in their rooftop beer garden. Or head to the Grosvenor Cinema, and split a bottle of wine between friends. Honestly, there's so much good stuff to choose from in this little lane that you can't really go wrong.

64 THE MEADOWS

Melville Drive
Edinburgh
EH9 1ND
mypark.scot/parks/meadows-edinburgh

The Meadows is one of Edinburgh's great green spaces and is a popular hang-out in summer evenings with BBQs, sports and other curricular activities happening. So grab a blanket, beers and some food and head to the Meadows like a proper local.

63 ASHTON LANE

Places
WORTH THE TRIP

65 **KNOYDART**
PH41 4PL
Highlands & Islands
visitknoydart.co.uk

Knoydart is a remote and magnificent community-owned peninsula on the west coast of Scotland. It's famous for being rather inaccessible: you can only get there by boat or on foot, after a 25-kilometre walk. Only 110 people live there, but they form a lively community that will make you feel most welcome. There's a community-owned bunkhouse that's open year-round, and the freshly renovated village hall has awesome music on once a month, even more in the summer months. Another valued space is the pub; the locals campaigned tirelessly to bring it under community ownership, as a way of investing in the regeneration and stability of the peninsula. So no more sitting outside to get eaten by the west coast midges! Knoydart is a special, unique place and well worth the trip.

66 ISLE OF EIGG

PH42 4RP
Highlands & Islands

Eigg is a magical place. A historical community buy-out took place in 1997: the islanders purchased the land back from an absentee landlord and the Heritage Trust was born. Nurtured back to its current glory the island is the first in the world to power its grid purely from wind, wave and solar energy; their supply is called Eigg Electric. The population of 105 is vibrant with plenty characters to get the *craic* with at the tearoom. The annual 'independence' *céilidh* in June is also not to be missed. White sandy beaches and views to the rest of the Inner Hebrides are simply breathtaking, with some of the best vistas from the summit of An Sgùrr and Laig Beach. Wildlife is also in abundance with seals, otters, sea birds and plenty wild flowers. If you're extremely lucky you can even sight orcas at the right time of the year. Contemporary bothies are a treat, but make sure to book well in advance. Take the Sheerwater Ferry from Arisaig for a more intimate crossing experience.

67 KINLOCH HOURN

Invergarry
PH35 4HD
Highlands & Islands

Kinloch Hourn is at the end of a 35,4-kilometre single-track road, which takes a bit of concentration, not just because of passing places etc, but because it's hard to keep your eyes on the road driving down this beautiful stretch. Head west from the A87 and turn off near Loch Garry. Kinloch Hourn is a sea loch, and almost fjord-like, with Ladhar Bheinn (the most westerly Munro on the mainland) shooting into the sky. When you get to the end of the road there is a jetty and a couple of car parks, one for overnight parking and one for day visitors. Why overnight parking? Well, because Kinloch Hourn is the doorway to the stunning Barrisdale Bay and Knoydart if you are up for the strenuous challenge.

68 ISLE OF GIGHA

Isle of Gigha
PA41 7AA
Argyll & Bute
+44 (0)1583 505 390
(Heritage Trust)
gigha.org.uk

Gigha is absolutely breathtakingly beautiful. It's the most southern of the Hebridean Isles and has been in community ownership since 2002. When you stand on this little island and look out, it feels like you are in the Caribbean. The white sandy beaches are just as spectacular as people say they are, and the water is clear and teal coloured, so take a snorkel mask, seriously! Just don't expect any coconuts, although you do get palm trees in Argyll due to the gulf stream. Original settlers on Gigha came from Ireland, and it was at the epicentre of conflict between Vikings and clan feuds. Norse King Hakon gave the island its name, *Gudy*, meaning good or God's Island. You can see why. There are lots of cycling and walking options to explore the island, so ditch the car and head to the famous Achamore Gardens, walk to the spouting cave or to one of the many beaches and enjoy the views over to Ireland, Islay and Kintyre. Make sure you try the Wee Isles ice cream and Gigha Oysters at the Boathouse, they're a must!

Cute COASTAL VILLAGES

69 **CROVIE VILLAGE**
Banff
AB45 3JQ
North

Crovie, pronounced *Crivie*, is a unique fishing hamlet between Macduff and Pennan. It started as a settlement during the 18th-century Clearances when estate owners cleared families from the land to make room for their sheep. The families had no other choice but to move to the cliffs and start to make a living from the sea. The fishing industry lasted until 1953, when a severe storm rendered the village pretty much useless. The most distinct thing about Crovie however is the access. It's so steep and narrow that it's inaccessible to cars, and residents have to carry their supplies by wheel barrow. Probably one of the most unique fishing villages in Scotland. Whilst you are here definitely check out Gardenstown and Pennan, too. And make a day of it.

70 PENNAN VILLAGE

70 PENNAN VILLAGE

Fraserburgh
AB43 6HY
North

Slightly further east from Crovie, you'll come to Pennan, another quirky fishing village that deserves a mention. The brightly coloured houses are vibrant on a blustery day and the listed red telephone box that featured in Billy Forsyth's blockbuster *Local Hero* is a must photo op! Pints at the Pennan Inn are class and well worth a stop. Not much more you can ask for from such a small village.

71 CARRADALE VILLAGE

Carradale
PA28 6RY
Argyll & Bute

Carradale is a lovely wee coastal village on the Kintyre peninsula, and is worth a stop if you're in the area. Get some ice cream at the Carradale Hotel and head down to the bay for an epic picnic spot. The Network Centre tells an interesting and important story about Carradale's close relationship to the sea, with its fishing industry and 'Steamie' trips that used to run up until the Second World War. Nearby Saddel Abbey is also super interesting with medieval stones, dating back to the 1300s, that are intricately carved, and a few believed to have been carved in Iona. Packs a punch for such a wee place.

72 FOOTDEE (FITTIE)

Fittie Village
Aberdeen
AB11 5DQ
North East

Footdee, or Fittie – as the locals call it, is a historical little fishing village on the south end of Aberdeen Harbour. The first settlement recorded at Fittie was in 1398, and the village steadily grew with its fishing prosperity being the main draw. The houses were designed in 1809 by renowned Aberdeen architect John Brown to rehome fishermen living locally in poor conditions. The homes were built in squares and initially in an identical fashion, which is what gives Fittie its unique feel, with narrow lanes and straight lines. In contrast to that, the 'tarry sheds' – originally built from driftwood and used to store fishing gear – are mismatched and awash with vibrant colours. A nice change in the Granite City. The welcome is warm in Fittie and it's a great place to grab an ice cream on the boulevard and watch the world go by. Although watch your food, Aberdeen seagulls are fierce.

73 VICTORIA HARBOUR

Victory Place
Dunbar
EH42 1HS
Lothians

Victoria Harbour is a charming little port in Dunbar, once one of the major herring and whaling ports in Scotland. At one side of the harbour you can find the ruined remains of Dunbar Castle and at the other side you can find an 18th-century fort and battery, which was prominent throughout the American Wars of Independence. Watch the commercial ships come in, mainly landing shellfish, and enjoy the atmosphere of this historical pier.

72 **FOOTDEE (FITTIE)**

74 **PLOCKTON**

74 PLOCKTON

IV52 8TP
Highlands & Islands
visitplockton.com

Some like to say that West is best, and you can see what they mean, especially when you get to Plockton. The village is situated in a sheltered bay overlooking the stunning sea loch, Loch Carron. Its pretty painted cottages and lively restaurants and bars give this place a great vibe. Although that hasn't always been the case. After the Highland Clearances and the end of the herring boom Plockton struggled immensely between 1850 and 1918 and was known as 'Village of the poor'. So it's nice to see the Highlands thriving again. There is loads to do: from biking to sea kayaking, exploring, and boat trips, and over 50 B&Bs to choose from.

ISLE OF MAY

EXPERIENCES

Great spots for **GOLF**

75 **MACHRIHANISH GOLF CLUB**

Golf Club Home
Machrihanish
PA28 6PT
Argyll & Bute
+44 (0)1586 810 213
machgolf.com

Famous for its picturesque and tough first hole, which requires your first shot to be played over the Atlantic, Machrihanish is one of the finest Scottish links courses we have to offer. The undulating greens, thick rough and unpredictable bounce of the links make this course a test for even the most proficient golfer. Excellent views over the beach and across to Islay, Jura and Ghiah. And for those not wanting to tackle the 'big course', the 9-holer is also a pleasure to play.

76 **CRUDEN BAY GOLF CLUB**

Aulton Road
Cruden Bay
AB42 0NN
North East
+44 (0)1779 812 285
crudenbay golfclub.co.uk

Cruden Bay is renowned for being one of the most spectacular and difficult links courses in Scotland. Ball positioning and good judgment will get you a long way here. If you are looking to brush up on your skills, head teaching professional Murray Patterson of MAPGolf will keep you right, and no doubt give you some local knowledge to get you playing that round you've always dreamed of. Good facilities and bar menu, too.

77 BLAIRGOWRIE GOLF CLUB

Golf Course Road
Rosemount,
Blairgowrie
PH10 6LS
North East
+44 (0)1250 872 622
theblairgowrie golfclub.co.uk

Forget the Rosemount and Lansdowne course, the Wee course at Blairgowrie is where it's at. Set in a beautiful pine and birch forest, which is lined with heather, it really is a little Scottish treasure. Just because it's wee, doesn't mean it's easy. The Par 3s and 4s will keep you on your toes.

78 KILLIN GOLF CLUB

The Golf House
Killin
FK21 8TX
Loch Lomond & Trossachs
+44 (0)1567 820 312
killingolfclub.co.uk

Killin is a beautiful little 9-hole course set in the beautiful hills of the Perthshire Highlands at the head of Loch Tay. The course has loads of character, and nothing will beat the local knowledge here with the ups and downs. Sure it's not a championship course in a traditional sense, but beauty is in the eye of the beholder.

Wee BREWERIES

79 FYNE ALES FARM BREWERY

AT: ACHADUNAN BUNGALOW
Cairndow
PA26 8BJ
Argyll & Bute
+44 (0)1499 600 120
fyneales.com

A great pit stop when heading through this area of Argyll. The brewery is situated on a working farm, and the once dairy barn now holds their brewery. Tours are available every day and last 40 minutes. Their bar stocks an amazing selection of cask, keg and bottled beers. They also have a great range of board games, which is nice on a rainy day. The pies made from spelt-grain-fed beef on the farm are another must try. And so is FyneFest, their annual music and beer festival.

80 TEMPEST BREWING

AT: TWEEDBANK INDUSTRIAL ESTATE, BLOCK 11, UNITS 1 & 2
Galashiels
TD1 3RS
Scottish Borders
+44 (0)1896 759 500
tempestbrewco.com

Tempest Brewing is creating some of the most exciting and delicious beers in Scotland. Based in Galashiels in the Scottish Borders, it's well worth the stop, especially if you are into craft beers. Tours are £10 and booking is essential, so please get in touch before you turn up. Drop Kick Me Jesus and Long White Cloud are amongst crowd favourites.

81 71 BREWING

36-40 Bellfield St
Dundee
DD1 5HZ
North East
+44 (0)1382 203 133
71brewing.com

71 Brewing is relatively new and the first brewery to surface in Dundee in over 50 years. It's an exciting place, housed in an old iron works. So the character and heritage of Dundee's industrial past are kept alive here, but at the same time the modern tastes in the beers reflect new beginnings. In the summer months they have a beer garden: it's a great place to grab a pint, like Mandarina Sky or Fruition Sours, to name some of the recommended labels here.

81 71 BREWING

GIN DISTILLERIES

worth a visit

82 EDEN MILL

Main St
Guardbridge,
St Andrews
KY16 0US
Central Scotland
edenmill.com

Eden Mill is famous for its premium craft gin served in their opaque bottles. Based in St Andrews, the distillery and brewing tours are a great way to spend a couple of hours when in the area. Their blendworks gin experience at the Rusack Hotel comes highly recommended, where you get to create and blend your own recipe of gin.

83 PERSIE GIN DISTILLERY

Glenshee Road, A93
Bridge of Cally
PH10 7LQ
North East
persiedistillery.com

Persie Gin Distillery is situated in the lovely hills of Glenshee and offers three gins in their traditional line-up. One is zesty, one herby and the other sweet and nutty. All three are distilled in small batches in the former Persie Hotel in Bridge of Cally. Their lovely staff will be more than happy to chat to you about their gin, with tours and tastings available. Booking essential.

84 BEINN AN TUIRC DISTILLERY / KINTYRE GIN

AT: TORRISDALE CASTLE ESTATE
Carradale,
Campbeltown
PA28 6QT
Argyll & Bute
+44 (0)1583 431 528
kintyregin.com

The Beinn an Tuirc Distillery is situated in the lovely Torrisdale Castle Estate on the east coast of the Kintyre Peninsula. The Kintyre gin uses botanics that reflect the unique coastal and woodland setting of the estate, which is powered completely by renewable energy. Bookings for tours are a must, and drivers get to take away a miniature for the road. For those of you who are being chauffeured, enjoy a G&T in a lovely part of the world.

Selected

WHISKY DISTILLERIES

85 **SPRINGBANK DISTILLERY**

9 Bolgam St
Campbeltown
PA28 6HZ
Argyll & Bute
+44 (0)1586 552 009
springbank.scot

Campbeltown used to be known as Whisky Capital of the World, with over 30 whiskies produced here. Only three distilleries now remain, with Springbank being the oldest independent family-owned distillery in Scotland, with the Mitchell family being 5th generation in. The distillery is housed in buildings dating back to 1828. It is the only Scottish distillery to have 100% of its production onsite and one of a handful of distilleries to keep the traditional floor malting methods. The tours are excellent and starting from £10, which includes a nip and a miniature to take away.

86 **EDRADOUR DISTILLERY**

Pitlochry
PH16 5JP
Highlands & Islands
edradour.com

Edradour Distillery was officially founded in 1825 by a cooperative of farmers, but dates back earlier and is steeped in illicit pot distilling history. It is the smallest distillery in Scotland and has stuck to its handmade and small-scale production roots, which only adds to the charm of this little distillery. Now back in Scottish hands – after ownership from larger cooperatives and the New York mafia – there are plenty of tales to be told on their guided tours.

86 **EDRADOUR DISTILLERY**

87 BALVENIE DISTILLERY

Dufftown
AB55 4BB
North
+44 (0)1340 822 210
thebalvenie.com

Balvenie is a very traditional distillery in Dufftown, where they keep centuries-old crafts close to their hearts. Founded in 1892, Balvenie still grow their own barley for malting in the fields that overlook the distillery. Once it is harvested, there are four other key components that are crafted on site that make Balvenie what it is: the traditional malting floor, the copper stills, the cooperage and the malt master. You can learn about all of these on their intimate tours, which are limited to 8 people. The Caribbean cask, which is aged in a rum cask, is definitely a talking point.

88 ABERLOUR DISTILLERY

A95, Banffshire
Aberlour
AB38 9PJ
North
+44 (0)1340 881 249
maltwhisky distilleries.com/ aberlour

Aberlour is one of the eight whisky distilleries that form Scotland's Whisky Trail, which is the largest concentration of whisky distilleries anywhere in the world, The location close to the river in the heart of Speyside adds to this small and friendly distillery's charm and to the whisky's quality, as water is drawn from nearby springs. Tours by knowledgeable staff are available, and if you're older than 18 there's an array of tastings, ranging from the best of Aberlour to a more exclusive Secret Speyside experience.

89 STRATHISLA DISTILLERY

Seafield Avenue
Keith
AB55 5BS
North
+44 (0)1542 783 044
chivas.com

Strathisla is a stunning distillery and the oldest working distillery in the Scottish Highlands. Its grounds are well manicured, its buildings quaint, and its tasting rooms grand. There are various tours to suit whisky novices and connoisseurs. One of the most unique is the blending experience where you can taste some of the special whiskies and make your own blend to take away.

Where to go for an **ADVENTURE**

90 ISLE OF MAY

BOAT AND TICKETS:
Anstruther Pleasure Cruises
Middle Pier
Anstruther
KY10 3AB
Central Scotland
+44 (0)7957 585 200
isleofmayferry.com

The Isle of May is a wonderful nature reserve in the Firth of Forth that's ideal for spotting sea birds such as puffins and mammals such as Atlantic grey seals. The best way to get over there is to book a boat trip with Anstruther Pleasure Cruises. The trips last around 4,5 to 5 hours giving you at least 2,5 hours on the island to enjoy the walks and scenery. The island is owned and maintained by Scottish Natural Heritage. They have rangers stationed there to give you important information about the island and its biodiversity. May and June are the best times to see breeding seabirds, and best to book later on in the day to see puffins, as they are usually out fishing during the day.

91 LOCH INSH

Kingussie
PH21 1NU
Highlands & Islands
+44 (0)1540 651 272
lochinsh.com

The Freshwater family have been providing adventure experiences at Loch Insh Outdoor Centre for over 50 years now. It is an epic place to spend the day taking up one of the many activities on offer, such as sailing, mountain biking, windsurfing, archery, kayaking…the list is endless! There is something for everyone and all abilities with instruction available. For those staying locally it's a great place to entertain the kids. On a sunny day the balcony is a perfect place to grab lunch, an ice cream or a beer at their restaurant. You can stay on site and there is an array of accommodation available.

90 **ISLE OF MAY**

92 GILMERTON COVE

16 Drum St
Edinburgh
EH17 8QH
gilmertoncove.co.uk

Hidden underground on the south side of Edinburgh, these passageways and chambers have been a mystery for hundreds of years. There are seven different rooms, each hand-carved. You can find a well, a fire place and a blacksmiths forge. Historians and archaeologists have studied the cove, but no clear purpose has been discovered or agreed upon. Some say it was a secret drinking den, others believe it was a witches' cove. Booking a tour is essential for these mystic caves.

93 CALUM'S SEAL BOAT TRIPS

32 Harbour St
Plockton
IV52 8TN
Highlands & Islands
+44 (0)1599 544 306
calums-sealtrips.com

Calum's Seal Boat Trips are a fantastic way to explore the seas of the west coast of Scotland. Calum, Jane and their crew have been running trips now for over 30 years and know the Plockton coastline like the back of their hands. The crew can't always guarantee seals, however the excursion is free if you don't see any. Join in on one of their special trad music cruises if you are looking for something different. All aboard the Sula Mhor for great memories!

93 **CALUM'S SEAL BOAT TRIPS**

ANGUS GLENS – CORRIE FEE

ADVENTURES

94 GLENLIVET MOUNTAIN BIKE TRAIL CENTRE

Kirkmichael
Tomintoul
AB37 9AR
Highlands & Islands
+44 (0)1479 870 070
glenlivetestate.co.uk

Glenlivet is an excellent trail centre that has something for everyone and great for kids. The blue trail is fun and perfect for beginners and the red trail offers something more challenging, but pedaly for the advanced riders. Both however have great vantage points for views across the glen. The flowy single tracks are situated in the heart of the Glenlivet Crown Estate and approximately 10 minutes away from Tomintoul. There's a cracking cafe, which is a great post-ride stop (check opening times on their website) with outside seating and a pump track, which is great to practise your skills or race your mates. Make sure to pay for parking, as the money goes back into maintaining the trails.

95 MORAY MONSTER TRAILS

Fochabers
IV32 7PG
North
+44 (0)300 067 6200
scotland.forestry.gov.uk

The Moray Monster Trails is a local trail centre in Fochabers that often gets overlooked but it is a great addition to the Scottish trail network. From the easier Ordiequish blue trails to the flowy and techy black Gully Monster, there is something suitable for all abilities. The fairly recent injection of cash to maintain and build a new skills area means it's a perfect spot to hone your skills and keep an eye on the kids. No toilets or cafe and parking open year-round.

96 GLENTRESS MOUNTAIN BIKE TRAIL CENTRE

Peebles
EH45 8NB
Scottish Borders
+44 (0)300 067 6900
scotland.forestry.gov.uk

Glentress is one of Scotland's flagship trail centres and is an excellent day out, especially if you have mixed ability groups. There are plenty of non-boring blue and skills loops to build confidence for newbies or perfect skills for those more experienced. The Tweed valley has hosted international events, so there's an abundance of world-class single track if you know where to look. The range of facilities also make it a great place to spend a day. The modern visitor centre has a good cafe, toilets and an Alpine bikes, which has a workshop, rentals and trail essentials. There is also a bike wash and shower block (shuts at 6 pm), which is great to wash away the day's muddy evidence.

96 GLENTRESS MOUNTAIN BIKE TRAIL CENTRE

97 COMRIE CROFT

Braincroft, Crieff
PH7 4JZ
Central Scotland
+44 (0)1764 670 140
comriecroft.com

Comrie Croft has got it all. Technical rock slab descents, flow trails, dual slaloms (so much fun!) and stunning views from the top. It's a great destination if you want to spend a full day. There are a bike shop and bike rentals, a workshop for any repairs and also coaches available, who provide kids' lessons in the summer. The team room is an epic cafe with great outdoor seating to grab good coffee, cakes and fresh food. For gentle family rides, there is a good path network taking you to St Fillans.

Amazing COASTAL WALKS

98 **SANDWOOD BAY**
Lairg
IV27 4RU
Highlands & Islands

Sandwood Bay is one of the most striking beaches in Scotland, right on the north-west tip. The bay is vast, beautiful and carpeted with red-tinted sand. You have to work for your reward though, as it's a 7,25-kilometre walk there and back, so allow yourself plenty of time. As you walk in, you'll follow a fairly flat path through mostly crofting land and past a few freshwater lochs. When you get to the beach, you'll be able to spot the Cape Wrath lighthouse on a clear day and the dramatic cliffs that form the coastline. The other feature to look out for is Am Buachaille, a giant Torridon sandstone sea stack that looms near the bay. Its name translates to 'The Shepard' from Gaelic. Park at Blairmore, and follow the path to one of Scotland's great wild landscapes.

99 SANDEND BEACH

Sandend, Banff
AB45 2UB
North

Sandend is a beautiful little fishing village between Portsoy and Cullen on the Moray Coast. Dating back to as early as the 1600s, the cottages are small, quaint and packed in giving it that classic seaside feel. The beach is great for swimming, dog walks and learning to surf. If you fancy giving it a shot, check out SUDS surf school. Follow the path east from the beach to locally known 'cup and saucer', which is the remains of an old windmill that stood until 1760 and was built on the site of an old burial cairn. It is situated beside Glenglassaugh Distillery. There are very few facilities in Sandend so you are best to take a picnic, or better still, pop your head into J Smith Fish Merchants, and see if you can get some of their amazing haddock.

100 RUBY BAY

Elie
Leven, Fife
KY9 1BS
Central Scotland

Ruby Bay is situated to the east of Elie on the Fife Coastal Path, and delivers a fantastic sandy beach and spectacular views out over the Firth of Forth. The bay is named after the type of garnet stone that is very occasionally found here. Lady Janet Anstruther's Tower is a special feature. They are remains of a bell tower that was erected in the 1770s as a changing room for her. When Lady Janet wanted to go for a swim, she sent a servant to ring the bell and let the people of Elie know to stay away from Ruby Bay. It's said she was ruthless of nature, and made a settlement move to improve the view from her house, which led to a curse being put on the family. Access by car on Wadeslea Road, or take the 20-minute-or-so walk from Elie. Toilets available.

101 DIABAIG COASTAL CIRCUIT

STARTING IN:

Lower Diabaig
IV22 2HE
Highlands & Islands

The Diabaig Coastal Circuit is a slightly more challenging coastal walk with excellent views over some of the north-west's most stunning lochs and hills. The complete loop is around 12,5 km with about 700 metres of climbing. It does get boggy in places and you should allow yourself at least 5 hours to complete it, 6 hours if you are wanting to go a slower pace. Recommended map for this area is OS Explorer Map (433) Torridon - Beinn Eighe & Liathach. Park in the small car park just before the pier, walk to the end of the road and go through the gate at Cadhanahearba cottage. Turn left immediately to another gate, through which you'll come to a small barn. The path bends here to the right and look out for a rock which has 'path' painted on it. Here marks the spot to the start of your adventure!

101 DIABAIG COASTAL CIRCUIT

Enchanting **WOODLANDS**

102 CULBIN FOREST

Kintessack
IV36 2TG
North

History of the Culbin can be dated back to the 13th century. It was acquired by the Forestry Commission in 1921 to replenish Britain's forests after WWI. If you head out to the shores you can find upright wooden poles that were placed in the ground to prevent enemy gliders landing here. The forest stretches over 17,3 kilometres hugging the coastline. Make sure you take a map or keep an eye on what trail you're on as it's easy to get lost in here. There are two car parks but Wellhill is the main one with toilets. Walking route 'Hill 99 trail' has a lookout tower with panoramic views of the stunning woodland and Moray Firth. Make sure you stop off at Wellhill farm shop on your way back to use their egg vending machine for the freshest eggs.

103 THE HERMITAGE

Old Military Road
Dunkeld
PH8 OJR
Highlands & Islands
+44 (0)1350 728 641
nts.org.uk

Perthshire is known as 'big tree country' and the Hermitage is one of the ideal locations to take in its natural beauty, especially in autumn. The lofty Douglas firs are amongst the highest trees in Britain and provide an enchanting woodland to explore. As you follow the trail you can hear the River Braan (which means roaring stream) as you approach, the water cascades over Black Linn Falls, which is best observed from Ossian's Hall balcony. Ossian's Hall is a folly built in 1757 to impress the Duke of Atholl's visitors. The original building was blasted to pieces in protest against tolls on the Dunkeld Bridge. The building you see now dates back to 1951 but has kept its impressive interior. Salmon can be seen migrating upriver in summer and autumn. A great way to break up the drive North on the A9. Parking £2.

103 THE HERMITAGE

104 KILLIECRANKIE

Pitlochry
PH16 5LG
Highlands & Islands
nts.org.uk

Killiecrankie is surrounded by fascinating nature and history. It was the site of an infamous Jacobite Rebellion Battle in 1689, led by Bonnie Dundee, where the Jacobites defeated government troops and sent the Redcoats packing. One government soldier in his desperate quest to escape the wrath of the Jacobite is said to have jumped the 18-feet gorge and survived. This spot is now known as Soldier's Leap. Garry Bridge further up provides another great vista spot in this stunning wooded glen. The glen has been designated as a site of special scientific research, due to its ancient woodland and the flora and fauna it attracts. Park at the visitor centre and pick up a trail map to follow the well-signposted routes.

105 ARDBLAIR TRAIL / BLUEBELL WOODS

61 Smithfield Cres
Blairgowrie
PH10 6UE
North East
pkct.org/blairgowrie-walks

Head here in spring to take in the beautiful bluebells of Perthshire. Give yourself between 2 and 2,5 hours to complete this 9,5-km circular walk that takes you on a lovely journey through woodland, countryside and past two small lochs. Start on Perth road and take the Ardblair Trail through Ardblair Wood. The path will then lead you to Darroch Wood, Gaelic for Oak Wood. Download a map from Perth & Kinross Countryside Trust before you go, as the tourist information is now closed. Please keep to the path so you don't squash the poor bluebells.

106 EAS MOR AND LOCH GARBAD

START: OPPOSITE CHURCH BRAE

Kildonan, Isle of Arran KA27 8SG Argyll & Bute

The Eas Mor woodland walk to Loch Garbad is a bonny trail that takes in a significant waterfall. Park in the designated car park opposite the road down to Kildonan. The start of the path is fairly smooth and leads to a forest above a steep-sided gorge. You'll continue higher and higher up where there are plenty of viewing platforms to take in the stunning landscape and the Eas Mor waterfall. You then finish at Loch Garbad, a calm hill loch, a great place to chill out. Find the charming turf-roofed eco library where there are books and drawings left by visitors. It's around 5,6 kilometres, so you should leave yourself 2 hours to complete.

107 GLENMORE FOREST PARK

Rothiemurchus, Aviemore PH22 1QU Highlands & Islands

Glenmore Forest provides endless opportunities to explore. From the ancient Caledonian pine forest, the magical Green Lochan, the Ryvoan Pass and the popular Loch Morlich. All in the foothills of the mighty Cairngorm Mountain range. This is a renowned location for spotting some of the UK's most-protected species including capercaillie, pine martens, red squirrels, crossbills, reindeer, golden eagles and if you're lucky, the odd ospreys flying overhead searching for their next meal. It's an important area for conservation because of the rich biodiversity, so that it is protected for generations to come. This really is one of Scotland's most incredible wild spaces, come here to connect with what's important.

108 ANGUS GLENS – CORRIE FEE

**Glen Clova,
Kirriemuir
DD8 4RD
North East
+44 (0)1575 550 233
(Ranger Centre)**
visitangus.com/glen-doll-ranger-centre

Corrie Fee has been shaped over thousands and thousands of years by the Ice Age and now leaves a stunning and rugged glacial *corrie* that's well worth the walk. *Corrie* in Gaelic means cauldron and you can see where it gets its name from. Its bowl shape provides a dramatic backdrop and access to some of the best of Scotland's wilderness. You'll also find rare Arctic flora and fauna here, such as the Alpine blue-sow-thistle amongst others. That's also why it qualifies as a National Nature Reserve and SSSI (Site of Specific Scientific Interest). Park at the Glen Doll car park and allow 2,5 hours for this 7,5-km walk. The paths are clearly marked, however check in at the ranger centre if unsure. There are also toilets available.

108 ANGUS GLENS – CORRIE FEE

109 BEN LAWERS NATIONAL NATURE RESERVE

CAR PARK: OFF A827 NORTH OF LOCH TAY
Killin
FK21 8TY
Loch Lomond & Trossachs
+44 (0)1567 820 988 (Ranger base)
nts.org.uk

Forget Ben Nevis, it's busy and full of tourists trying to tackle it in their flip-flops. Ben Lawers is where to go. Sitting at 1214 metres it is the 10th highest Munro in Scotland and it is a magnificent place to escape and take in nature, too. Red deer, ptarmigan and black grouse are just some of the wildlife you'll spot here. For those who don't want to walk to the top there are well-marked lower slope trails, but for those who want to take on the challenge and summit: please allow at least 6 hours to do so. Once you get to the top, breathtaking views await, especially over Loch Tay, Glencoe and over to the Cairngorms. It's really quite special. The National Trust frequently runs guided walks that are a great way to explore, especially for the less experienced. See their website for booking details. Please don't get caught out in the Scottish mountains, they are ruthless. So take walking essentials with you, even on a nice day. Park at the NNR car park and remember your £2 for parking.

110 PUCK'S GLEN

1,6 KM SOUTH OF BENMORE BOTANIC GARDEN
Benmore
PA23 8QT
Argyll & Bute
+44 (0)300 067 6600
forestryandland.gov.scot

Puck's Glen is a beautiful steep and narrow gorge that leads you through densely packed forest with lots of mosses and little waterfalls. It's darker in there, but that's what adds to the beautiful atmosphere. The glen is usually described as enchanting and you can see why within this Celtic rainforest. Tales in Scottish folklore say that fairies live here, such as Ghillie Dhu, a soft-natured mountain spirit that guards the trees. Watch your footing on the slippery stones when wet, and enjoy the circular walk.

111 COIRE FHIONN LOCHAN

North Ayrshire,
Isle of Arran
KA27 8HP
Argyll & Bute

Coire Fhionn is a beautiful wee mountain loch that sits about 350 metres above sea level. It's been carved out by glacial ice and now holds clear but peaty water fed by fresh hill streams. It even has its own little white granite beach, which is a great place to stop for a picnic, or to ditch your towel if you want to go for a dip. It's around a 5,6-kilometre walk, so it should take you a couple of hours to go there and back. The views over to the Mull of Kintyre on the way up are also beautiful. Park at Thundergay, which should get a laugh from the immature amongst us, and follow the signs.

112 CRAIGELLACHIE VIEWPOINT

AT: CRAIGELLACHIE NATIONAL NATURE RESERVE
Aviemore
PH22 1PR
Highlands & Islands
nature.scot

Start behind the YMCA Youth Hostel at the south side of Aviemore and use the tunnel to go under the A9. From there you'll follow a well-signposted route up to the summit. Before you get there though you'll have to make your way through the nature reserve, which takes in a pretty loch and birch woodland. Get to the summit cairn if you can, it provides epic panoramic views of the Cairngorms and the Spey valley that shouldn't be missed. If you walk a little further to the second cairn you'll get better views over to the west, and also spot another little lochan. Follow the same path back down, and reward yourself with a pint at the Old Bridge Inn afterwards. Allow 3 hours so you are not rushed.

113 URIE LOCH

Isle of Arran
KA27 8NU
Argyll & Bute

Urie Loch is an isolated hill loch 425 metres high on an open heather hill just below Tighvein. The track is short, but steep so it provides a good challenge. Once you get to the top you'll be rewarded with epic views over Lamlash Bay. The little grassy island in the middle is man-made to try and encourage red-throated diver birds to nest, just in case you were wondering. Park in the Dyemill car park, about 1,5 kilometre out of Lamlash and turn right at Monamore Bridge towards Kilmory, Isle of Arran.

114 LOCH CORUISK

BOAT OPTION:
Bella Jane Boat Trips
Elgol, Isle of Skye
IV49 9BJ
Highlands & Islands
+44 (0)1471 866 244
bellajane.co.uk

Loch Coruisk is in the heart of the magnificent Black Cuillin Hills and sits in a natural amphitheatre, which adds to the skyline's dramatic setting. The dark volcanic rock leaves big slabs, which add to the uniqueness of this stunning and remote area. The best way to reach Loch Coruisk is to take a boat from Elgol. There are a few providers, which can be easily researched online. The other access is the very long walk from Sligachan or Kilmarie, which require mountaineering skills to navigate safely, especially over the 'Bad step'. So needless to say you'll need to be very prepared for such an isolated area. However, the boat trip to Loch Coruisk adds to the charm and experience of exploring such a unique and serene part of Scotland's landscape. Oh, and wear good footwear, it can get slippery.

114 LOCH CORUISK

NEIST POINT – ISLE OF SKYE

LANDSCAPES

Bonnie **BEACHES**

115 WESTPORT BEACH

A83
Westport,
Campbeltown
PA28 6QD
Argyll & Bute

Westport Beach is a stunning beach on the Kintyre Peninsula, it stretches over almost 10 kilometres to Machrihanish and incorporates their famous dunes, which are an area of Scientific Interest (SSSI) because of the biodiversity they support. The rockpools are fun to play in and spot small fish and crabs. The Atlantic is popular with surfers, however beware if you are going in for a dip. Westport is renowned for its strong undercurrents, so read the sea and stay alert. Great place to come and stretch the legs or spend a sunny day. Park at the car park just eight kilometres north of Campbeltown.

116 MELLON UDRIGLE BEACH

Mellon Udrigle
IV22 2NT
Highlands & Islands

Before you reach the settlement of Mellon Udrigle you have to follow a narrow and twisty single-track road that leads you to the goods of the beach! Park at the clearly signposted car park and please don't park overnight here, but head to the campsite next door if that's your intention. Follow the wooden walkway to the famous silver sands of Camas a'Charaig Beach and take in the breath-taking scenery. The views over the water to Little Assynt, Coigach and Suilven Mountain make it extra special. Widely claimed to be the best stretch of land in Wester Ross, it would be a shame to pass and not experience it.

116 MELLON UDRIGLE BEACH

117 ISLE OF VATERSAY

Isle of Barra
HS9 5YW
Highlands & Islands

The Isle of Vatersay is small: approximately five by five kilometres. It lies just south of the Isle of Barra and is connected by a causeway. You'll find some of the most stunning white beaches here, and you can do a circular walk to link them all up and take in the stunning scenery. You can spot signs highlighting the past, from Annie Jane's monument to the WWII Catalina flying boat debris. There's so much to explore here, and it really is a beautiful place to escape, too.

118 OSTEL BAY

AKA: KILBRIDE BAY
Tighnabruaich
PA21 2AH
Argyll & Bute

Ostel Bay – also known as Kilbride Bay – forms a great crescent-shaped white sandy beach. The views over to Loch Fyne, Inchmarnock and Isle of Arran are wonderful. This spot deserves a bit of time, especially on a sunny day and provides a lovely mellow bathing spot. Not lots of facilities around, so best to come prepared.

120 **ACHMELVICH BAY**

119 BOSTA BEACH

Great Bernera, Isle of Lewis
HS2 9LT
Highlands & Islands

Bosta Beach is just one of the many outstandingly beautiful beaches in the Outer Hebrides. The white sand and turquoise water frequently get compared to more tropical places. It is definitely unique, but in this neck of the woods it is pretty standard issue! It's situated on the Island of Great Bernera, which is connected to Lewis by a bridge and has a fascinating history. In 1992 a severe storm exposed an ancient settlement dating back to the Iron Age. The excavated houses were all linked by underground tunnels, and one of them has been replicated, which you can explore and where you can learn more about this captivating area. Behind the beach lies the remains of the township Bostaidh, which was tragically cleared in the Highland Clearances around 200 years ago. Just offshore you'll notice the 'Time and Tide' bell, which is one of 12 and created by sculptor Marcus Vergette: the bell rings different notes at tidal times and is there to remind us of the threat of global warming and higher tides. A unique addition to a very unique place.

120 ACHMELVICH BAY

Lairg
IV27 4JB
Highlands & Islands

Achmelvich Bay is a fantastic beach on the west coast, with white sands and some excellent views over to the tops of unique-looking Suilven Mountain and rocky outcrops. Popular in the summer time with folks from the caravan sites, this is an excellent beach to enjoy on a sunny or brisk winter's day. Heads up, dogs aren't allowed during the height of the tourist season.

122 BOW FIDDLE ROCK

121 SILVER SANDS OF MORAR

Morar
PH40 4PA
Highlands & Islands

The Silver Sands of Morar are a collection of white sandy beaches that hug the coastline from Morar to Arisaig. Your eye follows the turquoise sea, up to the horizon where there are great views over to the small isles. There are little areas to pull over and enjoy the views, however the main parking is at Camusdarach, where you can jump out and enjoy the dunes. Please don't camp on the dunes, and damage the unique and fragile marram grass.

122 BOW FIDDLE ROCK

Portknockie
AB56 4JN
North

Bow Fiddle Rock must be the most charming rock on Instagram! It stands like the perfect life model, just waiting to be drawn and adored. It is a sea arch made of quartz sandstone, and given its name because it resembles the tip of a fiddle. It's a wonderful display of nature and worth a visit, and a photograph!

Dramatic LOCHS

123 LOCH MORAR

Morar
PH40 4PB
Highlands & Islands

Created over 10.000 years ago by the Ice Age, Loch Morar is the deepest freshwater Loch in the British Isles. It measures 310 metres or 1017 feet in depth and is 19,6 kilometres long and 1,6 kilometre wide, making it the fifth largest loch by surface area. Around the loch are superb views, and it provides a pretty backdrop to some of the area's best walks. There are three waymarked paths: Glasnacardoch to Lochs an Nostarie and Eireagoraidh, Bracorina to Tarbet and Allt an Loin to Loch a Bhada Dharaich. Make sure you have a map, as a couple of these trails are quite lengthy. You can often spot boats out on the loch fly fishing, usually for brown trout. Permits apply and there is a *ghillie* (meaning servant in Gaelic) service available to get a permit and to guide you. Fish by the rules of the *ghillie*! One of Scotland's great lochs.

124 LOCH TORRIDON

Torridon
IV22 2EY
Highlands & Islands

Loch Torridon is a vast and incredible landscape that takes in a few villages and townships on its 24-kilometre stretch. The Loch is a sea loch, and surrounded by magnificent Munros that arise from the sea, making this place a mecca for sea kayakers, hillwalkers and mountain bikers. Not to mention the famous Torridon sandstone that also attracts climbers. The bounty from the loch is also to be desired, with it producing top-quality Scottish seafood. One of the most beautiful spots in Scotland, it has plenty to offer and explore.

125 **KINLOCHEWE – BEINN EIGHE**

125 KINLOCHEWE

Achnasheen
IV22 2PB
Highlands & Islands

Kinlochewe and the wider Beinn Eighe National Nature Reserve (NNR) is an impressive stretch of land on Wester Ross. It was the first NNR established in Scotland in 1951 and in 2016 it was classified as a UNESCO Biosphere Reserve, acknowledging this area's importance internationally. The village of Kinlochewe is small, and the name suggests that it should sit at the head of Loch Ewe, which is puzzling because Loch Ewe is situated 24 kilometres north-west. However, in the 17th century the loch was renamed to Maree, in remembrance of St Maelrubha, who is recorded with bringing Christianity to Wester Ross. The visitor centre is only open during the summer months but is a great place to enquire about the area's many brilliant walks.

126 LOCHINDORB

Grantown-on-Spey
PH26 3PY
Highlands & Islands

Lochindorb's landscape has a beautiful but haunting feel to it, and that's no coincidence: Lochindorb translates to 'Loch of trouble' from Gaelic. It's a barren rolling landscape, and quite a change from the Cairngorm Mountains you pass arriving here. In the middle you can see ruins of a castle from the 13th century, which has troublesome tales to tell. It was occupied by the English in the Wars of Independence and Edward I of England visited here in 1303. It was occupied again in 1355 and used as a prison and garrison for English troops. Then at the tail end of the 14th century it was known as the 'Wolf's lair' as it was gifted to the ruthless Alexander Stewart aka The Wolf of Badenoch, who terrorised this part of the world. The landscape with its history makes Lochindorb a melancholic but captivating experience.

Lovely LOCHS

127 LOCH VAA

Aviemore
PH24 3BT
Highlands & Islands

Loch Vaa is a wee gem that, if you didn't know it was there, you would pass easily without thinking twice. It's a spring-fed loch, encased by a pretty pine and birch forest. It has a pebbly shore, which is great for stone skimming and often freezes in the winter, making it look like a winter wonderland. The red tin roof of the boathouse acts as a colourful contrast against the green of the forest and adds to the great charm of this landscape. In between Aviemore and Boat of Garten on the A95, park at Laggantrygown Cemetery and follow the clear path leading from the car park. However, this is the main cemetery for this local area, so please be respectful if there is a funeral going on, as it's not a very big car park.

128 LOCH AN EILEIN

Rothiemurchus, Aviemore PH22 1QT Highlands & Islands

Loch an Eilein translates to 'Loch of the island' where ruins of a castle lay, and it's one of the most picturesque lochs in Scotland. It's unknown for definite how old the castle is, but it is believed to be from the 14th century and was built for protection against the pillaging of clan feuds. The best way to observe is to walk the grand circular path, that takes you right round the loch and through some of Scotland's best natural landscapes. The pine woods are old and atmospheric and provide a backdrop for special flora and fauna. The great thing about Loch an Eilein is that it's very accessible, so suitable for small children, buggies and those who may be a bit slower than they once were. If you feel up for it, biking from Aviemore is also a great way to enjoy this picture-perfect loch. If you take the car: per person parking charges apply, so take cash.

127 LOCH VAA

Mighty GLENS

129 GLEN AFFRIC

Cannich
IV4 7LT
Highlands & Islands
forestryandland.gov.scot/visit/glen-affric

Glen Affric is one of the most beautiful glens in the land. It has one of the largest ancient Caledonian pine forests in Scotland and the Lochs Affric and Beinn a' Mheadhoin are perfect centre pieces to what Scots call the 'Shortbread tin' depiction of the Highlands of Scotland. Great walks through the nature reserve can be enjoyed, just drop in at the ranger service or refer to the Forestry commission's website for the most detailed trail maps. Colours of the glen are spectacular in the autumn, with trees and heather giving off lovely shades of orange and brown. But explorers beware! The mighty Highland midges are relentless and can be quite the distraction. So take a face net and a midge repellent. Or plan your visit when there is a bit of a breeze, or alternatively not in the height of the summer. One of Scotland's great Highland glens.

130 GLEN ETIVE

A82
Glencoe
PH49 4JA
Highlands & Islands

Glen Etive is just a simply stunning road off the A82 near Glencoe. This 22,5-kilometre single-track road leads to the head of Loch Etive and takes in some stunning scenery such as mountains 'The Buachaille' aka Buachaille Etive Mor, Ben Starav, and Stob Dubh. The glen is famous for its resident deer population. If you're lucky you can get your classic Highland stag shot. The River Etive is popular with whitewater kayakers, and has some mellow pools to dip in. But please do your research and assess the river, stay within your limits and apply common sense. As the glen has gotten more popular there has been an increase in littering, so please take your waste home with you and respect this gorgeous wild landscape. Locals' tip: don't go in the height of the tourist season, try and visit outwith that time and it will feel as if you've got the place to yourself. Also the film location for *Skyfall*, *Braveheart* and *Harry Potter*, you'll understand why when you visit.

131 SPITTAL OF GLENSHEE

Blairgowrie
PH10 9QF
North East

The A93 is one of Scotland's most beautiful roads to drive. The Spittal of Glenshee is where four glens meet, and it provides some classic Highland vistas. Your onward journey will lead you to Royal Deeside or the Cairngorms National Park. You can link these together and take a route called the Snow Roads. In Gaelic it's called *Gleann Shith,* meaning Glen of the Fairies, and you can see why as it's a magical place.

130 GLEN ETIVE

132 BEALACH NA BA PASS

Strathcarron, Applecross
IV54 8XF
Highlands & Islands

Bealach na Ba Pass is not for the faint-hearted! It's an 18-kilometre rollercoaster of a mountain road with sharp hairpins, very steep inclines and passing places to negotiate. The views are stunning, but the road deserves your full attention. And it's not suitable for large motor homes, caravans and learner drivers. Just don't do it. Built in 1822, its name translates to 'pass of the cattle' from Gaelic, and was used to drive cattle over this mountain terrain. On the other side, the delights of Applecross await.

133 QUEEN'S VIEW

Pitlochry
PH16 5NR
Highlands & Islands
forestryandland.gov.scot

Queen's View might be a popular tourist stop, but it's all for good reason. The viewpoint looking up Loch Tummel and over to Schiehallion is impressive, and on a very clear day you can even spot the mountains surrounding Glencoe. When Queen Victoria visited here with her loyal servant John Brown in 1866, she assumed the view was named after her, however it's believed to be named after Robert the Bruce's first wife Isabelle, who lived 550 years earlier. To escape the buses and occasional selfie stick, go very early in the morning or later on in the afternoon. You can also quickly escape other tourists by exploring the beautiful Allean Forest nearby. All trail info available at the visitor centre, where there are also toilets and a cafe.

132 BEALACH NA BA PASS

Lofty LIGHTHOUSES

134 ARDNAMURCHAN PENINSULA

Ardnamurchan
Point
PH36 4LN
Highlands &
Islands

Ardnamurchan is the most westerly point on the British mainland and sits on a remote peninsula. The two main ways to access are by taking the Corran Ferry just south of Fort William on the A82. It's a short trip across Loch Linnhe to Strontain, where you'll join the single track. Or take the A830 road from Glenfinnan and turn off on the A861 at Lochailort, which will add on about an hour. Whatever way you choose, they are both beautiful, and will take you down the long and windy single track showing off some of the best scenery on the west coast. Once you get to Ardnamurchan Point, there is a great lighthouse to visit that was built in 1850 and is an impressive 36 metres high, with a cafe and exhibition. Sanna Bay is a perfect location to take in the remote beauty of this spot. You also get an interesting view over to the Inner Hebrides, to the An Sgùrr on Eigg and the mountains of Rum.

135 NEIST POINT LIGHTHOUSE

Isle of Skye
IV55 8WU
Highlands & Islands
isleofskye.com

Neist Point is the most westerly point on the Isle of Skye and it's where this lighthouse is perfectly placed to protect seafarers passing through the strait of Minch. It stands an impressive 43 metres above the sea and is remotely operated in Edinburgh by the Northern Lighthouse Board. It was designed by Robert Louis Stevenson's cousin, David Alan Stevenson, in 1909. The last lighthouse keeper left in 1990 due to automation and it is now derelict. Park in the car park and follow the well-constructed path, it should take you around 45 minutes. Heading here at sunset is incredible, but just remember your head torch.

135 NEIST POINT LIGHTHOUSE

Wandering **WATER**

136 FALLS OF FALLOCH
Crianlarich
FK20 8RL
Loch Lomond & Trossachs
lochlomond-trossachs.org

Falloch Falls is also known as the 'hidden falls' (as they translate into Gaelic) or Rob Roy's bath tub! They provide an excellent backdrop for a stopping point if travelling up and down the A82. Or a picnic spot, but please take your rubbish away with you! It is also a great swimming hole, but only for confident swimmers. The 10-metre jump is a bit much if you're still in arm bands. John Kennedy's installation *Woven Sound* is a great place for a photo and gives a new perspective on the falls, with the cantilever view point made of woven steel. It's a busy stop in the summer so the car park can get full. If it does, please don't park on the A82, it's illegal and can cause an accident.

137 FALLS OF FOYERS
45 B852
Inverness
IV2 6XX
Highlands & Islands

The Falls of Foyers is a grand waterfall about 50 metres high and feeds the famous Loch Ness. In Gaelic it means the 'smokey waterfall' and it's a nice feature to enjoy, along with the wooden gorge. Stop off if you're looking for a little detour off the busy A82.

138 PLODDA FALLS

Cannich, Beauly
IV4 7LY
Highlands & Islands

During your exploration of Glen Affric, Plodda Falls is definitely a little highlight and has some great acoustics, as you can get up close. It's 46 metres high, and has a viewing platform that extends out from the top cliff, providing a good photo spot and bird's eye view. It's just a bit further up (approximately 8 kilometres) from the little village of Tomich along a narrow road and forest track, but it's worth the adventure.

139 INVERMORISTON FALLS

River Moriston
Inverness
IV63 7WE
Highlands & Islands

Just north of Fort Augustus these pretty falls have a nice vantage point and short wooden walks to enjoy the area. The best way to appreciate them is from the Thomas Telford Bridge, built in 1813 and formerly the main crossing from Drumnadrochit to Fort Augustus. The water is usually at its most rapid on Tuesday when they release the Dundreggan dam.

140 BURN O'VAT

Dinnet
AB34 5NB
North East

Burn O'Vat also known as McGregor's Cave is a glacial pothole that was created 16.000 years ago. When the glacial ice (also know as the vat) melted it caused a cascade of water to carry debris and boulders, until one of the boulders got stuck and the water needed to flow around it, causing this 13-metre-high and 18-metre-wide hole. It's an interesting formation and cool to explore. It was once a hiding place for the notorious Pádruig Mac Griogair (Patrick McGregor) who was a fugitive and famous 17th-century cattle robber. Visitor centre and toilets available. Also great walks around the area.

141 FALLS OF SHIN

B864
Lairg
IV27 4EX
Highlands & Islands

The Falls of Shin are an epic place to come and spend an afternoon or morning as there is plenty to keep you entertained. The visitor centre is run by the Kyle of Sutherland Development Trust and includes a nicely stocked shop and a great food joint run by Mac and Wild. The burgers are excellent! Definitely no stale overpriced sandwiches here. That's all before you've properly explored. The River Shin is a famous spot and arguably the best place to watch the wild Atlantic salmon migrate. The best time to see them is in the summer. There is a minigolf, a playground and some great woodland walks in Achany Forest that are accessible to adventurers and those who want to take it more mellow.

139 INVERMORISTON FALLS

Must-visit

NATURE RESERVES

142 ST CYRUS NATIONAL NATURE RESERVE

Montrose
DD10 0AQ
North East
nature.scot

This often-windy nature reserve is a great place to blow away the cobwebs. The sand dunes offer some relief and protect the grasslands, which means in summer there is a lovely burst of colour with wild flowers. The vast beach makes you feel small and is a great place for birdwatching. The view from the cliff tops near the village end isn't bad either. Visitor centre with toilets is available.

143 MUIR OF DINNET NATIONAL NATURE RESERVE

Burn O'Vat
Dinnet
AB34 5NB
North East
nature.scot

Once you've explored the granite cauldron of 'the vat' the Muir of Dinnet Nature Reserve has great walks and a mixture of lochs and wetlands and woodland. You can spot all kinds of fauna and flora here: from the famous Scots pine to the mythical rowan and willow trees, as well as over 140 different bird species that have been recorded here. There have been several archaeological finds here too, with a 9th-century pictish stone, a logboat and an Iron Age crannog (free-standing wooden structure). All of this combined makes it a great place to go for an exploration.

AULDEARN ANTIQUES

SHOPPING

BOOKSHOPS *with character*

144 **ARMCHAIR BOOKS**
72-74 West Port
Edinburgh
EH1 2LE
+44 (0)131 229 5927
armchairbooks.co.uk

Getting lost down the rabbit hole is quite an enjoyable experience at Armchair Books. Books are bursting from what seems like every corner of the shop, which is bound to give any organisational enthusiast a slight heart attack. But you don't come here for the latest bestsellers, perfectly organised displays and Costa Coffee. You come here to get stunned by the eclectic choice and the books that seem to be as old as Edinburgh itself. Go get lost.

145 **LEAKEY'S BOOKSHOP**
Church St
Inverness
IV1 1EY
Highlands & Islands
+44 (0)1463 239 947

Leakey's secondhand bookshop possesses an amount of character and charm that you think is only attainable in the fairy-tale books it sells. Housed in a Gaelic church dating back to 1793, this sanctuary now provides space for a different type of worship. The high ceilings, pulpit and log burning stove are just part of what make this place so special. A definite stop for book lovers.

146 CALTON BOOKS

159 London Road
Glasgow
G1 5BX
+44 (0)7547 743 303
calton-books.co.uk

Based near the famous Barras on London Road, Calton Books is Glasgow's Independent Radical Bookshop, run by volunteers. The literature here promotes the local working-class history and joins the dots around the world to embrace other working-class ideas, politics and history. The stuff you 'weren't taught in school'. Radical free thinking is encouraged here and you can choose from genres such as feminism, anarchy, Marxism, civil rights and refugees to name a few. T-shirts, pins, patches amongst other things are also available.

144 ARMCHAIR BOOKS

147 VOLTAIRE AND ROUSSEAU

12-14 Otago Lane
Glasgow
G12 8PB
+44 (0)141 339 1811

Get sucked down Otago Lane and into another dimension at Voltaire and Rousseau, which has stood as a secondhand bookstore for over 40 years. The sea of stacked books seems to go on and on and on. You get the feeling that in this new dimension the book chooses you, not the other way around. Give yourself time to sift through, as it will beat ordering a book off Amazon any day of the year.

More great BOOKSHOPS

148 **GOLDEN HARE BOOKS**
68 St Stephen St
Stockbridge
EH3 5AQ
Edinburgh
+44 (0)131 225 7755
goldenhare books.com

Golden Hare Books has been carefully created to capture creativity, curiosity and community. The shop is cosy, the staff are knowledgeable and regular events are scheduled to draw in book lovers from all ages and backgrounds. They're well worth keeping an eye out for. Time is only restricted to what you allow yourself. Taking time to pick your next book is encouraged and you never feel rushed or pressured to purchase, so enjoy the browse and the excitement of selecting your next read. International shipping is also handy if you want to travel light and have your holiday purchases waiting for you when you get home. They also record a podcast, if that's your kinda thing.

149 **ORB'S BOOKSHOP**
33-A Deveron St
Huntly
AB54 8BY
North
+44 (0)1466 793 765
orbsbookshop.co.uk

Access to literature shouldn't be based on your ability to pay, but on your ability to read. That is why community bookshops like Orb's are so important. Selling everything from collector's items to bestsellers and 20-pence secondhand books, there is something accessible for all. The staff are all volunteers and will be willing to suggest your next read, and fill you in on the backstory of why it's so important to support their (and your) community through books.

150 THE EDINBURGH BOOKSHOP

219 Bruntsfield Place
Bruntsfield
EH10 4DH
Edinburgh
+44 (0)131 447 1917
edinburghbookshop.com

Situated in Bruntsfield, this is a great place to pick up a new book and head to one of the many cafes or 'the links' on a sunny day to enjoy your new purchase. Opened in 2007 the Edinburgh Bookshop has a diverse selection to choose from and is a specialist children's bookseller. Storytime runs every Thursday and Friday from 9.30 am for under-5-year-olds, a fun way to spend a morning whether you're local or visiting. Enjoy the warm welcome and interesting suggestions from the staff.

151 ATKINSON-PRYCE BOOKSHOP

27 High St
Biggar
ML12 6DA
Glasgow
+44 (0)1899 221 225
atkinson-pryce.co.uk

This is a grand wee bookstore on the High Street of Biggar. You'll pass here if you're going east to west or vice versa on the A702 and it's definitely worth a stop. Great Scottish selection and the staff are very friendly, not to mention their hilarious chalkboards. There is a reason this bookshop is award winning.

152 THE HIGHLAND BOOKSHOP

60 High St
Fort William
PH33 6AH
Highlands & Islands
+44 (0)1397 705 931
highlandbookshop.com

The Highland Bookshop is an excellent addition to the Fort William High Street and their warm tartan carpets invite you in. Given its location in the 'Outdoor Capital' of the UK, you can find a superb selection of outdoor and local books, amongst others. Head along to one of their events, as they usually draw in some great names. Get inspired for your next adventure here.

153 THE WATERMILL

Mill St
Aberfeldy
PH15 2BG
Highlands & Islands
+44 (0)1887 822 896
aberfeldy watermill.com

This bookshop, art gallery and cafe blend together and offer a unique experience inside an old renovated watermill dating back to 1825. The bookshop is award winning and has lots of interesting local books, some of which have been published in house. The gallery upstairs has a unique rotating display of art, prints and ceramics. Food in the cafe is a delight, with generous healthy portions of soup, salads and rustic seeded rolls with quality fillings. Sitting out on the deck in the summer and enjoying their mix platter is also advised.

BIKE SHOPS *to check out*

154 **RIDE SCOTLAND**
AT: RAILWAY STATION
Boat of Garten
PH24 3BH
Highlands &
Islands
+44 (0)1479 831 729
ridescotland.com

Founded by local shredder Nash Masson, Ride Scotland will have you covered for all your mountain bike needs. Based beside the old Strathspey Steam Railway station (that's still in operation) in Boat of Garten, it's certainly one of the prettiest bike shops in Scotland. Kids and adult bikes are available to hire plus tag-along trailers for those wee ones who aren't big enough 'to go a bike' yet. A good selection of e-bikes is also available to hire, great for those who haven't been on a bike in a while, wanting some assistance or looking to cover lots of ground. Don't miss Chopstick the chow, maybe the cutest shop assistant ever.

154 RIDE SCOTLAND

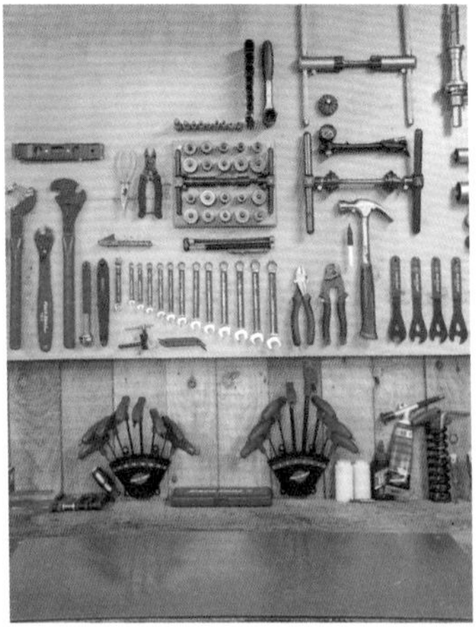

155 BASECAMP BIKES

5 The Square
Grantown-on-Spey
PH26 3HF
Highlands & Islands
+44 (0)1479 870 050
basecampmtb.com

You'll always get a warm welcome and honest answers out of owner Lindsey and Ben at BaseCamp Bikes. Bike hire is available for children and adults, and if you are hiring for more than two days the guys will deliver your bikes to your door, which is super convenient. E-bikes are also available. If your bike is in need of some tender loving care, then BaseCamp has got the extensive knowledge and workshop to get you up and running again, their servicing goes recommended amongst the engaged local MTB scene. Good selection of retail for a small shop, which is handy if you've forgotten your gloves, helmet or waterproof jacket... or just want to treat yourself! Coffee also available, best to take your own cup and ask Ben to make you a flat white, he perfected his craft in NZ!

156 CYCLE HIGHLANDS

AT: THE PAVILLION
Victoria Road
Ballater
AB35 5QQ
North East
+44 (0)1339 755 864
cyclehighlands.com

Rich and his team are in an excellent place to gear you up and send you exploring around the beautiful Royal Deeside and Ballater area. Bike sales and hire available with your own little skills loop outside. Guiding service is also offered by qualified leaders, which is a great way to get the best out of the local area. Nice selection of retail with workshop to keep you rolling.

Places for **VINTAGE** *finds*

157 **AULDEARN ANTIQUES**

Dalmore Manse,
Lethen Road
Auldearn, Nairn
IV12 5HZ
+44 (0)1667 453 087
auldearn antiques.co.uk

A family-run business for over 25 years, this is a great find just outside the sleepy village of Auldearn. Secondhand furniture, china, bric-a-brac, vintage clothing and architectural items are spread out across the beautiful buildings. From lofty large spaces, to little cosy rooms. You're always due a warm welcome at Auldearn Antiques, and remember one man's trash is another's treasure. Go find yours.

158 **W. ARMSTRONG & SON**

83 Grassmarket
Cowgate
EH1 2HJ
Edinburgh
+44 (0)131 220 5557
armstrongs vintage.co.uk

Starting life in 1840, this well-established vintage clothing and accessories store has been delighting customers through the eras. Packed with clothing from the 1950s through to the 1990s, what was once in fashion, then out of fashion is now back in fashion! As the rails are adorned with a wonderful assortment of colours and fabrics to sift through at reasonable prices. A mecca for those who want unique and one-off garments that no one else will have. With the current trend to reject fast fashion, Armstrongs have been well ahead of their time. They have three shops in Edinburgh with each one having its own personality, however the Grassmarket location deserves a special mention.

157 AULDEARN ANTIQUES

158 W. ARMSTRONG & SON

159 STARRY STARRY NIGHT

19 Dowanside Lane
Glasgow
G12 9BZ
+44 (0)141 337 1837
starrystarrynight vintage.co.uk

Tucked down a cobbled lane, this little vintage shop can provide some gems. Opened in 1986, the shop offers lots of styles to flick through, from Victorian all the way to the 1980s. It's well worth a visit if you are looking for something unique that can't be found on the high street.

160 CONCORDE MUSIC

15 Scott St
Perth
PH1 5EJ
Central Scotland
+44 (0)1738 621 818
concordemusic.com

This little record shop packs a punch with a wide variety of mediums to choose from. The vinyl collection ranges from 12" singles and 7" singles to secondhand records from all different types of genres. This is also Scotland's oldest independent record store, established in 1967. Go and have a look, there is something to suit all tastes.

Looking for A BEVVY?

161 **THE WHISKY CASTLE**

6 Main St
Tomintoul
AB37 9EX
Highlands & Islands
+44 (0)1807 580 213
whiskycastle.com

The Whisky Castle is something of an institution and a world-class retailer that has been going for over 100 years. Their team are friendly and have excellent suggestions for your taste and budget, so don't shy away, especially if you're new to the party. There are over 600 malts and many of them are independently bottled, making them unique and exclusive to the Castle. Tastings are available for free. And bigger groups can be accommodated but best to phone ahead. Great and relevant stop on Scotland's Whisky Trail.

162 **VALHALLA'S GOAT**

449 Great Western Road
Glasgow
G12 8HH
+44 (0)141 337 3441
valhallasgoat.com

Valhalla's Goat is based in the trendy West End and stocks an amazing selection of craft beers, spirits and wines. If you're into craft beer at all, this bottle shop really reflects the quality and diversity of Scotland's exciting brewing scene. There are plenty choices from further afield as well, but it's great to have such a large selection of Scotland's finest. Keeping with what Scotland does well, there is also a fine selection of gin and whisky. The clued-up staff will be able to help you select what's right for your taste and your wallet. It's a great independent bottle shop if you're looking for something the beige supermarket selection can't offer.

163 THE CARNEGIE WHISKY CELLARS

Castle St
Dornoch
IV25 3DF
Highlands & Islands
+44 (0)1862 811 791
carnegiewhisky cellars.co.uk

Based in the old Carnegie Courthouse, this whisky retailer is one of a kind. It focusses on local distilleries but has a wide variety of distinct whiskies from across Scotland on offer. The knowledgeable staff can direct different tastings and master class experiences in gin and whisky to test your knowledge and learn more about our national industry. Set in their lovely tasting room.

NOT TARTAN TAT *shops*

164 THE WEE GIFT SHOP

42 Church St
Troon
KA10 6AU
South
+44 (0)1292 319 984
theweegiftshop.com

This is a great studio shop that showcases the best of Scottish creativity, sustainability and ethics. The carefully curated selection includes items by local creators such as jewellery, prints, homeware, cosmetics, and more. Owner Gayle opened the shop in 2020 and is very committed to giving back to the local community, so it's nice to know you're supporting small and local businesses as you shop.

165 GEEK BOTHY

1 High St
Kemnay, Inverurie
AB51 5NB
North East
+44 (0)7881 206 329
geekbothy.co.uk

The Geek Bothy is a multi-award-winning independent gift shop based in Aberdeenshire. Family run and stocking over 70 local creators, there are some really unusual and quirky treasures to be found, including a great selection of pocket money toys that keep the kids excited, and crafting kits for those who are into DIY. They also host maker-run workshops in their studio for all ages and abilities.

166 ÒR

4 Wentworth St
Portree, Isle of Skye
IV51 9EJ
Highlands & Islands
+44 (0)1478 613 444
orshopskye.com

A shop so good they've got two! One is on Wentworth Street, and the other on The Green in Portree. Focussing on Scottish contemporary gifts, the selection is beautiful, modern and high quality. ÒR really offers the opposite of the mass-produced trinkets that you get elsewhere – time and care have gone into the collaborations and the result is definitely worth seeing for yourself.

167 HIGHLAND STONEWARE

Lochinver
IV27 4LP
Highlands & Islands
+44 (0)1571 844 376
highlandstoneware.com

Highland Stoneware was started in 1974 and is now one of the biggest employers in Lochinver, with locations both there and in Ullapool. Each of their 24 staff contributes to the design process, adding their own style and taking inspiration from their beautiful surroundings, and there is an option to personalise designs if you have the time to wait. You can also pick up bargains in the second-chance shop.

168 THE ROLLING RAIL

AT: ROTHIEMURCHUS CENTRE
Aviemore
PH22 1QH
Highlands & Islands
+44 (0)1479 812 345
rothiemurchus.net

This pop-up shop is open in the summer months; it's run by Nancy McKenna, a local curator and costume designer and stylist who has worked on big-budget movie and TV sets. Showcasing both contemporary and vintage clothing, cosmetics and accessories, all selected with sustainability in mind, this is a great stop if you're looking for something different for yourself or the kids. An awesome addition to the popular Rothiemurchus The Barn.

169 HATCH

340 W Prince's St
Glasgow
G4 9HF
hatchglasgow.co.uk

By independent designers, for independent designers – that is the ethos at Hatch, and it shows in their selection of ceramics, textiles, jewellery, illustrations and gifts. Aside from the retail space with items by more than 100 UK designers. there is also a workshop space for artist-led workshops, if you fancy trying something different. Definitely check out their social media to see if they have anything going on. A great wee shop.

Shops for NICE FINDS

170 DICK'S

3 NW Circus Place
Stockbridge
EH3 6ST
Edinburgh
+44 (0)131 226 6220
dicks-edinburgh.co.uk

You can tell time and love have gone into curating the selection at Dick's by owners Uli and Andrew. Their ethos of sourcing garments and pieces from independent quality manufacturers shines through. Care and craft are important here, as to buy cheap is to buy twice. So if you want to invest in something you will adore and admire for years to come, Dick's is the place to go.

171 NICHE OPTICAL TAILOR

119 Candleriggs
Glasgow
G1 1NP
+44 (0)141 553 2077
nicheoptical tailor.co.uk

Not your normal run-of-the-mill opticians. Stocking everything from the weird to the wonderful in reading specs and sunglasses, this optical shop is a great place if you are looking for a visual upgrade. Stocking independent designers, you're bound to pick something just as individual as yourself.

172 KARTEL

9 Church St
St Andrews
KY16 9NW
Central Scotland
+44 (0)1334 479 333
kartel.co.uk

This cool contemporary watch shop in St Andrews is a flagship store for the Scottish brand Kartel. Their pieces reflect the modern and classy designs coming from Scottish designers using traditional fabrics such as Harris Tweed. You can also customise your watch with engraving, which is another nice touch if you are looking to mark a special occasion or special holiday.

173 THE MAINSTREET TRADING COMPANY

Main St
St Boswells
TD6 0AT
Scottish Borders
+44 (0)1835 824 087
mainstreet books.co.uk

The Mainstreet Trading Company is much more than just an independent bookshop. This old auction house now includes an excellent cafe, deli and home department. You'll find various items that have taken time and care to select, with an emphasis on supporting independent suppliers and artisans, which is evident in everything from their cheeses to their stationery. The children's book section should also get a special mention, and the creative window displays that draw you in.

174 SUBVERSION GALLERY

57 Ruthven Lane
Glasgow
G12 9BG
+44 (0)141 237 5575
subversion gallery.co.uk

Located in Unit 4 at Ruthven Mews, Subversion specialises in bringing pop art and urban art to the West End of Glasgow. Opened in 2015, Subversion has something for both the modest and flush budgets. They state that life is too short for boring walls, and their collection certainly backs that up.

175 APPLECROSS PHOTOGRAPHIC GALLERY

Camusterrach,
Applecross
IV54 8LU
Highlands & Islands
+44 (0)1520 744 395
applecrossgallery.com

A little gallery set up in a disused telephone exchange which exhibits stunning prints and canvases of the north-west scenery by local Jack Marris. Free coffee as you browse. Check opening times outwith the height of the season.

175 APPLECROSS PHOTOGRAPHIC GALLERY

Where to go for
QUALITY PRODUCE

176 I.J.MELLIS

330 Morningside Road
Edinburgh
EH10 4QJ
+44 (0)131 661 9955
mellischeese.net

The quality and variety of artisan cheeses here is excellent. As far as cheesemongers go, this is top class, as I.J.Mellis have been trading for over 25 years. Quality over mass quantity is what's important here, with knowledgeable staff and a traditional shopping experience making it a special place to visit. Cheese lovers, stock up here.

177 BOWHOUSE MARKET

AT: BALCASKIE ESTATE
St Monans,
Anstruther
KY10 2DB
Central Scotland
+44 (0)1333 720 200
bowhousefife.com

Bowhouse wanted to plug that gap between farm and fork, and has created a dedicated space each month, where the best producers and growers can get in front of the public who are looking for the best-quality produce. You can expect a lovely atmosphere in a covered space, so you can take your time and enjoy, even in the wettest of days. Coffee roasters, organic veg, artisan breads, fish, oils and quality-butchered meat is just some of what you'll find here. A foodie heaven.

178 ISLE OF MULL CHEESE

AT: SGRIOB-RUADH FARM
Tobermory,
Isle of Mull
PA75 6QD
Argyll & Bute
+44 (0)1688 302 627
isleofmull cheese.co.uk

The family-run business produces award-winning cheese on the Isle of Mull. Their own herd is milked in the morning on Sgriob-ruadh Farm and sent straight over to the cheese-making vat. You can then experience the maturing stage in their cellar. The glass garden barn is brilliant, serving up their artisan cheese amongst other fresh options on the menu and the farm shop stocks quality produce that should definitely be taken home.

179 AUCHENTULLICH FARM SHOP

Arden, Alexandria
G83 8RF
Loch Lomond & Trossachs
+44 (0)1389 850 240

You could drive by Auchentullich a hundred times and not realise what a gem you've passed. This foodie family are fifth-generation dairy farmers who decided to diversify in 2012. The result is terrific, with fresh locally sourced veg, cheeses, and Highland beef reared on the farm. Their ice cream is also excellent with unusual flavours like sea buckthorn and cranachan. In the winter they serve mulled wine heated on top of a wood-burning stove. Adorable! Not to be missed when passing on the A82.

INVER

FOOD

SEAFOOD *shacks & chippies*

180 LOBSTER SHACK

Harbour Lodge
North Berwick
EH39 4SS
Lothians
+44 (0)7910 620 480
lobstershack.co.uk

Open seasonally, the Lobster Shack is an awesome pop-up for seafood lovers at the heart of North Berwick's harbour. The little shed offers up sustainably caught seafood as they are registered as a 'first-sale fish' buyer, which means they source produce straight from the boats in the harbour as they land. The outside seating provides great views and plenty of fresh sea air to get the full experience. The lobster and chips are definitely to be sampled and washed down with either a beer or a glass of prosecco depending on how fancy you're feeling. The portions are small though, so great for a snack rather than a big meal. May-October.

181 SKIPNESS SEAFOOD CABIN

Skipness, Tarbert
PA29 6XU
Argyll & Bute
+44 (0)1880 760 207
skipnessseafoodcabin.co.uk

This Seafood Cabin is right beside Skipness Castle. The family-run business serves up basic seafood done well. The seafood platter is definitely a goer. The seating area gives you plenty of benches outside to enjoy your picnic and a licensed bar is available. Scottish seafood with Scottish castles, you can't get it more epic!

182 MARA FISH BAR & DELI

Shore Road
Corrie,
Isle of Arran
KA27 8JB
Argyll & Bute
+44 (0)1770 810 555
mara-arran.co.uk

Freshly decorated with a modern maritime look. *Mara* means the sea in Scots Gaelic. Nothing short of amazing, this seafood takeaway. New and exciting menu ideas that are impressing the locals and tourists on the Isle of Arran. Serving Dear Green, a speciality coffee roasted in Glasgow. Vegan options available. Breakfast and lunch only. No booking required.

183 THE FISH MARKET (TAKEAWAY)

23-A Pier Place
Newhaven
EH6 4LP
Edinburgh
+44 (0)131 552 8262
thefishmarket newhaven.co.uk

This is posh fish and chips. Fish is sustainably sourced from Welch Fishmongers next door and gives you plenty to choose from, like lemon sol, cod, haddock, monk fish and even deep fried crab claws are on the menu. You don't have to have your fish traditionally battered and fried though, as they can bread crumb or grill it for you, which is a nice change. Check out the specials board as they usually have something different on that's worth trying. Not to mention their different dipping sauces from Vietnamese to aioli and homemade tartare. Or as you're in Edinburgh it be rude not to have the traditional salt 'n' sauce. Expect to wait on glorious summer evenings, but the seating outside provides a great spot to watch the Newhaven sunset. Or go early and catch their oyster happy hour from 5 to 6 pm if that's your thing.

184 CATCH FISH AND CHIPS

186 Fenwick Road
Giffnock
G46 6XF
Glasgow
+44 (0)141 638 9169
catchfish andchips.co.uk

Glaswegians love their takeaways but this chippy certainly shines through. Offering king scallops, fish pakora, lobster and prawn rolls this certainly isn't your normal chip shop. Sit-in available with an eclectic beer and wine selection to match. Visit their other venues in Netherlee and the West End.

185 ANSTRUTHER FISH BAR

42-44 Shore St
Anstruther
KY10 3AQ
Central Scotland
+44 (0)1333 310 518
anstruther fishbar.co.uk

Anstruther is famous for its fish and chips and this chip shop is the main reason. Fishing history runs in the blood of the shop owners. A few years ago they won the UK's Seafood Fish and Chips Award. The staff are dressed in traditional white pinnies and white caps giving it a vintage feel. Perfect location right by the harbour so get a takeaway and sit beside the water but be prepared to fight off the local seagulls! This place is very popular so expect a queue out the door.

CHEAP *eats*

186 **CHEESE & TOMATIN**
10 Stephens Brae
Inverness
IV2 3JN
Highlands & Islands
+44 (0)1463 223 752

Cheese & Tomatin is a family-run affair producing delicious wood-fired Neapolitan pizza in Inverness. The dough might be rooted in Italy but the toppings are Scottish fare! With black pudding and haggis making a debut, not to mention the other great fresh choices. Keep an eye out for them on the road, as you might spot them with their pop-ups at events.

187 **THE PITT**
125-137 Pitt St
Leith
EH6 4DE
Edinburgh
+44 (0)7534 157 477
thepitt.co.uk

Down an unassuming lane just up from the water of Leith you'll find The Pitt, named after the street it is on, Pitt Street. This once old yard has now been given a new lease on life with a cool range of street food, drinks stalls and live music (think busker style). Perfect for summer vibes and in the colder months there are fire pits to cram around. Usually on once a week with a suggested donation of £2 entry. You could easily spend the afternoon in this small hip hang-out. Also check out their food and flea alternative market in Edinburgh's old town.

188 CLARK'S 24 HOUR BAKERY

3 Annfield Road
Dundee
DD1 5JH
North East
+44 (0)1382 641 048
clarksbakery.co.uk

Dundee institution Clark's 24 Hour Bakery is now in its third generation. Starting in 1950 this bakery has been a haven for clubbers, commuters, students and everyone in between. Their mouth-watering pies have to be sampled if you are in Dundee, especially after the pubs close. You can choose from traditional fillings such as macaroni, steak, and tattie bean. Or more adventurous ones like chicken tikka, bolognaise or sweet rhubarb pie. But whatever choice you go for, order "*Twa hoat pehs an an ingin ane ana*". That means: "Two hot pies and a onion one as well" for those who don't know.

189 BROSS BAGELS

177 Portobello
High St
Edinburgh
EH15 1EU
+44 (0)131 629 1860
brossbagels.com

Started by eccentric owner Larah Bross, the mission was simple: bring the best bagels to Scotland. Which Bross and her team have successfully done. The Montreal bagels are a delicious quick snack, with plenty of amazing fillings to suit the vegans, veggies and carnivores amongst us. Get involved! Their location in Portobello is great for a bagel and a stroll down the beachfront.

188 **CLARK'S 24 HOUR BAKERY**

SWEET TOOTHS' *favourites*

190 **OVER LANGSHAW ICE CREAM**
Grassmarket (police box)
Edinburgh
EH1 2AW
+44 (0)1896 860 687 (Farmhouse)
overlangshawfarm.co.uk

On a hot day (or not) this little police box in the heart of the Grassmarket is a great place to stop, grab an ice cream and watch the world go by in one of the most fascinating parts of Edinburgh. The ice cream is made in the Scottish Borders at the Over Langshaw Farmhouse, and is flavoured with local seasonal berries and no artificial stuff. The farm is powered renewably by their turbine called 'Winifred' and the gooseberry sorbet is an awesome choice for vegans. Save yourself the wait at Mary's Milk Bar, and report in at this wee police box.

190 OVER LANGSHAW ICE CREAM

191 TANTRUM DOUGHNUTS

27 Old Dumbarton Road, Yorkhill
Glasgow
G3 8RD
+44 (0)141 339 9319
tantrum doughnuts.com

Doughnut shops seem to be popping up all over the city these days, but this one is worth a visit. Glasgow has a long, complicated history with sugar but there is only pure enjoyment here. All the doughnuts are handmade and the dough is left to rise for 16 hours to obtain the best flavour. Their homemade marshmallows are a must-try. You can also check out their second location on Gordon Street, which is not far from Glasgow Central and perfect for a treat in the centre of town.

192 BAD GIRL BAKERY

Great North Road
Muir of Ord
IV6 7TP
Highlands & Islands
+44 (0)1463 872 734

Situated in the Forbes Buildings in the small town of Muir of Ord – 9 miles west of Inverness – you'll find this genuinely magnificent cake shop and bakery, taking a refreshing look at modern-day baking. It would be rude not to treat yourself here, sweet or savoury.

193 JANNETTAS GELATERIA

31 South St
St Andrews
KY16 9QR
Central Scotland
+44 (0)1334 473 285
jannettas.co.uk

Janettas is something of a St Andrews institution, and with fame come long lines in the summer, but it's all for good reason, so don't be put off! The wait is totally worth it. Janettas serves over 100 flavours, so there is something for everyone. It's a perfect addition to wandering around St Andrews, or an ideal treat after a day on the golf course.

194 MACKIE'S 19.2

7 Marischal Square
Aberdeen
AB10 1BL
North East
+44 (0)1224 518 252
mackies.co.uk

In most supermarkets in Scotland, if you head to the frozen section, you'll be able to spot Mackie's of Scotland ice cream with its blue and cream tub. Well this Aberdeenshire farm, famous for its ice cream, has opened its first parlour in Aberdeen and it's worth a shot! There are plenty of flavours to choose from, but the most notorious is the haggis and marmalade! *Affa fine.*

Where to go for the BEST CATCH

195 GILLE BRIGHDE RESTAURANT
Lower Diabaig
IV22 2HE
Highlands & Islands
+44 (0)1445 790 245
gille-brighde.com

This once was an old schoolhouse tucked away in the dramatic scenery of Loch Torridon. This is local seafood and produce at its best. A lot of thought has been put into the food here from sea to land to plate. Friendly welcome and Highland hospitality here. Opened from Easter until the end of October with then still limited opening times so please check and book before your visit.

195 GILLE BRIGHDE RESTAURANT

196 THE OYSTER-CATCHER

Otter Ferry,
Tighnabruaich
PA21 2DH
Argyll & Bute
+44 (0)1700 821 229
theoystercatcher otterferry.co.uk

Head down this long and winding single-track road until you eventually come to The Oystercatcher. It has a beautiful pontoon outside that must be a hit with sun baskers and bathers alike in the summer, or for those who enjoy a cold dip. Admittedly, the building looks unassuming from the outside, but what happens inside is what matters. With new owners Phoebe and Steve, it's great to see the pub continue its upward trajectory. The interior has a modern, spacious but cosy pub-feel to it, with rustic wooden furniture and panelling. The menu is superb, with everything made in-house and carefully paired. There are lots of fresh fish choices, veggie options, and Ballimore oysters from Loch Fyne, which the pub overlooks. The bar stocks an array of Scottish craft beer, with lots of really nice options to try. The Oystercatcher is well worth the detour, or even a destination in itself.

196 THE OYSTERCATCHER

197 **THE SHIELDAIG BAR & COASTAL KITCHEN**

Shieldaig
IV54 8XN
Highlands & Islands
+44 (0)1520 755 251
shieldaigbarcoastalkitchen.co.uk

The outside seating and upstairs deck provide an amazing setting to watch the world go by in one of Scotland's most scenic settings on Loch Torridon. Specialising in local seafood and wood-fired pizza, this bar is a perfect stop-off if you are in the area. Local An Teallach Brewery on tap for ale lovers and not a bad selection for a wee bar. Get the *craic* on Saturday nights as they usually have a folk session on the go, which is worth popping your head in the door for. Booking advised at the height of the season.

197 VIEW FROM THE SHIELDAIG BAR AND COASTAL KITCHEN

198 THE APPLECROSS INN

Shore St
Applecross
IV54 8LR
Highlands & Islands
+44 (0)1520 744 262
applecrossinn.co.uk

When you drop down from the dramatic Bealach na Ba Pass you continue to follow the famously twisty road until you reach a T-junction and turn left to the acclaimed Applecross Inn. The outside seating provides excellent views over the water to Raasay and Skye. The observant types amongst you might even spot lurking submarines in the distance. The menu is famous for its seafood, but other fine Scottish options are available, and in big portions. The bar has a good selection of real ales, whisky and gin. During the height of the season it is very popular, so best to keep dining times flexible. If not, head to their retro food truck 'The Inn-side out' for fish and chips. If you use the community Wi-Fi please make sure to contribute a donation.

198 THE APPLECROSS INN

HARBOUR *eats*

199 **CAFÉ CA'DORA**
Harbour St
Tarbert
PA29 6UD
Argyll & Bute
+44 (0)1880 820 258

Smack bang at the harbour front in the lovely Tarbert, Café Ca'Dora serves up Scottish cafe classics. From breakfast rolls and paninis to seafood. Simple but works.

200 **CAFE FISH**
The Pier, Main St
Tobermory,
Isle of Mull
PA75 6NU
Argyll & Bute
+44 (0)1688 301 253
thecafefish.com

Not many fish restaurants can say they own a fishing boat called The Highlander! No wonder this partnership made in heaven works so well. With the constantly changing special board depending on the catch of the day, which lands at 4 pm, you know you are in for a treat. Being situated on the top floor of the Calmac Pier gives this space one of the best views of Tobermory Bay. A must-try are the Croig oysters – caught off the Mull coastline – and the Sound of Mull scallops. Booking is essential. Open from March until October.

201 THE BOATHOUSE

Isle of Ulva
PA73 6LZ
Argyll & Bute
+44 (0)1688 500 241

If you fancy a bit of island hopping then the Isle Ulva is definitely worth a visit, just off the coast of Mull. The Boathouse is at the ferry terminal and will greet you when you arrive. They really care about their food here and don't cut corners. The locally rope-grown oysters and lobster caught by the family fishing boat make it extra special, just like your visit to Ulva.

202 STARFISH RESTAURANT

Castle St
Tarbert
PA29 6UH
Argyll & Bute
+44 (0)1880 820 733
starfishtarbert.com

The Starfish's exterior wouldn't go amiss in the Mediterranean with its white walls and bright blue shutters. Quality seafood is on the menu, which is caught locally and some landed at the Tarbert harbour just a stone's throw away. They have a great wine list to pair with your food and the friendly staff will happily advise. Booking advised and closed during the winter months.

MEAT-FREE *meals*

203 **HARMONIUM**
60 Henderson St
Leith
EH6 6DE
Edinburgh
+44 (0)131 558 3536
harmoniumbar.co.uk

This fully vegan restaurant was much anticipated in Edinburgh and it doesn't disappoint. Delivered by the team behind the popular Mono in Glasgow, the menu is varied and offers everything from 'juicy quarter pounders' (actually seitan) to creamy pastas and stone-baked pizzas. The bar also has a great selection of craft beers, great cocktails with daily specials and a completely vegan wine list. Set in a historical Leith location, this place is reasonably priced and great for an animal-free evening.

204 **THE HUG AND PINT**
171 Great
Western Road
Glasgow
G4 9AW
+44 (0)141 258 2882
thehugandpint.com

Pub slash amazing vegan food slash live music venue... what more do you want people?! This little West End hang-out is great if you are looking for healthy, Asian-inspired sharing dishes in a cool but not pretentious setting. There is no set menu, which keeps it fresh and interesting. The bar has a good choice of craft beers and there is decent live music on most nights.

205 MONO

12 King's Court
Glasgow
G1 5RB
+44 (0)141 553 2400
monocafebar.com

Mono set the standard for vegan food in Glasgow. This restaurant, bar and live music venue is bound to offer you a great night. The space is open, alternative and a pleasure to be in. The high ceilings and shape offer interesting acoustics for gigs and their independent vinyl shop next door provides the soundtrack to your visit. The tofu fish and chips is pure vegan comfort food and the rest of the menu has something for everyone from pizzas and curries to burgers. The bar has an excellent choice of craft beers, soft drinks and an organic wine list. Hipster? Maybe. Good? Definitely.

206 THE WILDCAT

21 High St
Fort William
PH33 6DH
Highlands & Islands
wildcatcafe.co.uk

The Wildcat is a revelation for vegans living in or visiting the Highlands. Situated in Fort William's High Street this cafe has great-quality produce and sustainability at its core. The big windows, high ceilings and alternative decor add to the good vibes. The coffee is something to look forward to and the tea menu is extensive. All milks are plant based, so try something different as the staff will be happy to help you choose if you've never tried one before. Their menu serves up great hearty soups, perfect after a morning on the hill, and other organic options. Don't let the fact that this place is 100% vegan put you off, as you'd be missing one of the best spots in Fort William. There is also a small plastic-free wholefood shop up the back, which is great for stocking up guilt-free. Also don't forget your re-usable coffee cup if you want to take away, as they don't have a disposable one to give you.

207 PILLARS OF HERCULES

Falkland
KY15 7AD
Central Scotland
+44 (0)1337 857 749
pillars.co.uk

Established in 1983 this organic farm, shop and cafe have been ploughing the ethical route for a few years now. The organic farm's starting principles were to produce great-quality products with a minimal impact on the environment. The cafe has good coffee and a veggie and vegan menu – what better way to sample the farm's produce. Lots of outside seating, ideal for a sunny day, and camping available.

PUB GRUB *places*

208 **THE ROSELEAF**

23-24 Sandport Place
Leith
EH6 6EW
Edinburgh
+44 (0)131 476 5268
roseleaf.co.uk

Run by Jonny and his lovely team, The Roseleaf is a cosy and laidback pub on the shores of Leith. The decor is quirky and you can't miss the mix-and-match of hats placed around the rooms which are perfect to try on when drinking their 'pot-tails', their cocktails served in teapots and your granny's best china. The menus are British pub food, done really well. You can choose to sit in the livelier front where the bar is, or at the back. But wherever you sit, make sure you head down for their awesome brunch, paired with a Bloody Mary to ease that whisky hangover from the night before.

209 **THE SCRAN AND SCALLIE**

1 Comely Bank Rd
Stockbridge
EH4 1DR
Edinburgh
+44 (0)131 332 6281
scranandscallie.com

If fine dining and pub grub had a baby, out would pop The Scran and Scallie. Started by renowned Scottish Michelin-starred chefs Tom Kitchen and Dominic Jack, this Stockbridge pub delivers quality classic dishes such as bone marrow steak pie, lamb rump and a Sunday roast, which are brilliant. The interior is tastefully done with tartan and tweed and the bar offers up great seasonal cocktails, craft beer and traditional pub bevvys.

210 THE COURIE INN

Main St
Killin, Perthshire
FK21 8UT
Loch Lomond & Trossachs
+44 (0)1567 831 000
thecourieinn.com

You are guaranteed to receive a warm welcome here. The Courie Inn is a great place to eat, sleep and drink in the fabulous scenery of Loch Tay, not far from the falls of Dochart. The menu features traditional Scottish cuisine that won't disappoint. You can eat in the lounge bar or bistro but the latter is recommended to book. The rooms are tastefully decorated and perfect for resting up after a day out exploring.

211 THE DORES INN

B862
Dores
IV2 6TR
Highlands & Islands
+44 (0)1463 751 203
thedoresinn.co.uk

On the south shores of Loch Ness you'll find this traditional Scottish charming pub and restaurant. Soak up the sun in summer with its scattered picnic benches around the inn and even onto Loch Ness Beach. They offer a shuttle bus free of charge within a 10-mile radius (essential to book). Homecooked Scottish food. In the winter opening hours are reduced.

211 THE DORES INN

212 THE COBBLES

7 Bowmont St
Kelso
TD5 7JH
Scottish Borders
+44 (0)1573 223 548
thecobbleskelso.co.uk

This old inn hides just off the main street and offers a relaxed place to grab some food, how a pub should be. They offer first-class bar meals and pour local beers, so be sure to sample the exciting local Tempest Brewing. Head here on a Friday night for the Kelso folk sessions.

214 THE OLD BRIDGE INN

213 THE STEAMBOAT INN

Carsethorn
Dumfries
DG2 8DS
South
+44 (0)1387 880 631
steamboatinn.co.uk

This seaside pub has an Aladdin's cave of bar memorabilia and artefacts. The location is idyllic in its own microclimate of the Solway coast. Locally sourced food and they are not stingy with the portions. You'll be welcomed off the beach here in any weather, with a roaring fire or beer garden, whatever the day demands. Check out their BBQ and smoker.

214 THE OLD BRIDGE INN

Dalfaber Road
Aviemore
PH22 1PU
Highlands & Islands
+44 (0)1479 811 137
oldbridgeinn.co.uk

The author's favourite local pub in Scotland (so maybe slightly biased). The Old Bridge Inn has plenty in store for a great night. The seasonal menus are delicious and of high quality. Scott's cocktails are rival to if not better than swanky cosmopolitan joints in the city, and the Guinness is not bad either. The inn provides outside seating by the River Spey and a live music roster that will bring you some of the best electronic DJs or folk musicians in Scotland. Popular with locals and tourists, so book dinner to avoid disappointment. Dogs allowed.

FOODIES' *choices*

215 **GARDENER'S COTTAGE**

AT: ROYAL TERRACE GARDENS
1 London Road
Edinburgh
EH7 5DX
+44 (0)131 378 7990
thegardenerscottage.co

The name Gardener's Cottage describes what it once was. This cute little cottage is right in the heart of Edinburgh in Royal Terrace Gardens and was built in 1836. As you are walking up to the entrance you can spot the vegetable and herb patches that yield the produce that the chefs use for their excellent dishes. The menu is all about sourcing the best possible local seasonal produce in a sustainable way and it really pays off, as their dishes are exceptional. The cocktail list shouldn't go amiss either. The dining is communal and admittedly not for everyone, however if you are open-minded and up for mixing in with other guests then this is a special dining experience.

216 **NUMBER 16**

16 Byres Road
Glasgow
G11 5JY
+44 (0)141 339 2544
number16.co.uk

This place impresses with a menu of European intertwined with Scottish cooking. The chefs know what they are doing here with beautiful presentation. They have made use of the small space available by having a mezzanine, which works really well with the modern stylish interior. Open for lunch and dinner, booking is advised. Perfect for a date night.

215 **GARDENER'S COTTAGE**

217 THE KILBERRY INN

Kilberry
PA29 6YD
Argyll & Bute
+44 (0)1880 770 223
kilberryinn.com

The white stone walls and red roof give this croft house a quaint look that fits in so well with its west coast surroundings. Awarded the 'Michelin Bib Gourmand' for high-quality cooking at a reasonable price. The food here is the reason why this place is a destination in itself with touches like their in-house smoking. The five bedrooms are named after the local islands and are stylishly furnished. The interior of the restaurant is striking with its exposed croft stone, open fire and rustic beams. Run by pair Clare and David you are sure to have an exceptional time here. Dinner, bed and breakfast is the best way to appreciate their full experience. Booking essential.

218 SIX BY NICO

1132 Argyle St
Glasgow
G3 8TD
+44 (0)141 334 5661
sixbynico.co.uk

This concept restaurant is clever, fun and a unique way to spend your evening. The six-course tasting menu changes every six weeks. Past themes have included the 1970s, Mexico, Childhood and Forest. Nico and his team wonderfully manage to incorporate each theme into each course. Go and surprise yourself and step into the world that Nico and his team have created just for you.

219 FIVE MARCH

140 Elderslie St
Glasgow
G3 7QF
+44 (0)141 573 1400
fivemarch.co.uk

You'll find nothing boring on the menu here. Using an array of ingredients that work together to deliver a treat for the senses, Five March is a pleasure to dine in. Beautifully presented dishes and an intriguing cocktail menu. Not to be missed.

220 THE HOEBRIDGE

Hoebridge Rd East
Gattonside
TD6 9LZ
Scottish Borders
+44 (0)1896 823 082
thehoebridge.com

You will be impressed straight away by their truly elegant space. The fresh white walls, arches and beams make the furnishings and fittings stand out. The food is delicious, well constructed and beautifully presented. Guaranteed you'll want a second visit. The cocktail list is full of classics, because that's sometimes all you need. If it's a nice day, sit in their secluded garden.

221 THE KALE YARD

AT: BOATH HOUSE
Nairn
IV12 5TE
Highlands & Islands
+44 (0)1667 454 896
boath-house.com/the-kale-yard

Just outside Nairn the newly opened Kale Yard is situated in the already well-established Boath House. Set in the beautiful walled garden, this sleek modern building fits in well. This offers more of a relaxed dining experience compared to the main house, but is still just as memorable. The wood-fired oven produces some fantastic pizzas Friday and Saturday, and the Italian theme continues with their pasta Thursdays. Menu is written daily on an authentic paper roll. Sit outside and enjoy the escape the garden provides.

222 THE CAPON TREE TOWN HOUSE

61-63 High St
Jedburgh
TD8 6DQ
Scottish Borders
+44 (0)1835 869 596
thecapontree.com

This part of Scotland can sometimes be overlooked, but is well worth exploring. This boutique hotel offers contemporary seasonal dishes and recently won the 'French Restaurant of the Year in Scotland 2018' award. Its teal walls and crisp white tablecloths act as a nice contrast, and light bites are served from 2 pm onwards.

223 INVER

Strathlachlan,
Strachur
PA27 8BU
Argyll & Bute
+44 (0)1369 860 537
inverrestaurant.co.uk

Chef Pam's laugh is infectious, genuine and transcends into the menu here. It doesn't take a professional food critic to understand the care, quality and curation that has gone into each plate, and the beautiful results it produces. All experienced in a relaxed setting with a great drinks lists and views over to Old Castle Lachlan to match. You can book their luxury en-suite bothies to turn your visit into the destination it deserves. Just don't call them pods.

223 **INVER**

224 **THE WALNUT**

9 Croall Place
Edinburgh
EH7 4LT
+44 (0)131 281 1236
thewalnut edinburgh.co.uk

The Walnut on Leith walk is what British bistro food should be and feels like your mum's cooking, but better. Lots better. The small space means that you have to book a table to guarantee a spot. Don't let the underwhelming interior put you off, it has no reflection on the food. When you arrive, you are encouraged to study a menu that is written daily on a big black chalkboard, which feels like a commitment to keeping it fresh and interesting. BYOB with a small corkage fee is also an added bonus to the already pleasurable experience. Excellent value for money given the quality. If you want a weekend treat, get in on the Sunday roast, it's not to be missed.

225 **THE SANDDOLLAR CAFE & BISTRO**

2 Beach Esplanade
Aberdeen
AB24 5NS
North East
+44 (0)1224 572 288
sanddollarcafe.com

Right on the Aberdeen beach promenade, The Sanddollar is a bistro cafe perfect for early breakfast (served from 7 am until 2 pm), lunch and – if you're lucky – dinner. Thursday to Sunday this cosy cafe turns into a classic seaside bistro with white linen, candles and a locally sourced menu to match. It's a perfect spot to unwind and come and enjoy good food.

226 **BUCHANAN BISTRO**
AT: WOODEND BARN
Banchory
AB31 5QA
North East
+44 (0)1330 826 530
buchananfood.com

Next to creative space the Barn arts centre, Buchanan Bistro offers wonderfully innovative and sustainable cooking. Their allotments provide ingredients for their menu, and the pickling and smoking are done on site. Lots of great veggie, vegan and gluten-free options. The friendly knowledgeable staff will be able to keep you right. The Bistro has lovely floor-to-ceiling windows and a spacious feel, but is kept warm by their fairy lights in the evening. Definitely give it a try if you are in the Banchory area.

227 **GORDON CASTLE CAFE**
Fochabers
IV32 7PQ
North
+44 (0)1343 820 244
gordoncastle.co.uk

Gordon Castle Estate has a lot to offer. The walled garden has been beautifully restored to its former glory, which dates back to the 15th century. Enjoy a fresh seasonal menu dictated by their garden, with their ethos being 'plant, pick and plate'. They make their own gin here, aptly named Gordon Castle and also have a children's play area… Perfect!

228 **CAFE LEPHIN**
2 Lephin
Glendale,
Isle of Skye
IV55 8WJ
Highlands & Islands
+44 (0)1470 511 465
cafelephin.co.uk

Lovely little family-run cafe on the way to Neist Point Lighthouse in Glendale. Great coffee, homebakes and fresh cafe food. They also stock a small range of art and artisan creations that are a lovely touch, especially if you are looking to take something unique home with you.

INSTAGRAM - *worthy hang-outs*

229 CAFE STRANGE BREW

1082 Pollokshaws Road
Glasgow
G41 3XA
+44 (0)141 440 7290

The hipster hype is real. Laurie and her staff have created a wonderful brunch and coffee spot with some of the most Instagrammable dishes around. Situated in the up-and-coming Southside, expect to wait (especially at weekends). The menu serves up brunches with influences from around the world but with using the best of Scottish produce. The Turkish eggs with garlic yoghurt and pomegranate are recommended and so is their creamy salmon baked egg with asparagus. Interior nods its head to Glasgows classic tenement style with the revealed tiles, giving it that warm and homely feeling.

230 SIMPSONS CAFE

27 Exchange St
Dundee
DD1 3DJ
North East
+44 (0)1382 203 950
simpsonscafe.co.uk

This trendy but not overly pretentious cafe offers breakfast, brunch, lunch and coffee. The light-bulb chandeliers, evergreen tiles and brightly patterned wallpaper give this place a chic feel. Owned and run by three generations of the Simpson family this ethically minded and sourced business gives you a lot to look forward to. They even recycle coffee grinds to use on Granddad Bill's vegetable allotment in Newburgh, Fife. Their food is carefully presented, with bursts of colour and brunches served in individual skillets. Try their BMBLT with Puddledub bacon, their own Bloody Mary tomatoes, rocket and housemade chipotle chilli mayo.

231 FOODSTORY

13-15 Thistle St
Aberdeen
AB10 1XZ
North East
foodstorycafe.co.uk

Community is at the heart of Foodstory. Started in 2013 by a Kickstarter campaign this cafe is much more than just coffee and cakes. A community space, zero waste shop and commitment to sustainability without the patronising is what you'll find here. Most of the furniture has been donated or salvaged giving it a DIY-inspiring feel that transcends into their menu. The food is healthy, locally sourced as much as possible and mostly veggie to keep up their commitment to environmentalism. They serve a good cup of coffee, too.

231 **FOODSTORY**

THE BEN NEVIS BAR

DRINKS

232 **TCHAI-OVNA**
42 Otago Lane
Glasgow
G12 8PB
+44 (0)141 357 4524
tchaiovna.com

This speciality tea shop stocks over 100 teas. You'll find it down a small cobbled lane just a short walk from Kelvinbridge Station. The building was originally an old stable, giving it an authentic teahouse feel with the soft furnishings and the menu inspired by far-flung places. The food however is sourced as locally as possible, and they are working with local suppliers and artists. The menu is all vegetarian or vegan and there is no alcohol sold here. They often hold creative events such as drama, storytelling and art exhibitions, which are popular with the local student population.

232 TCHAI-OVNA

233 THE HIDDEN LANE TEA ROOM

1103 Argyle St
Finnieston
G3 8ND
Glasgow
+44 (0)141 237 4391
hiddenlane tearoom.com

This tiny yet bright tearoom is tucked away in Unit 8 of the area known as Hidden Lane in Finnieston. Its vintage theme and mix-and-match crockery add to that special afternoon tea treat, which they stack up traditionally on a cake tier.

234 MUNEROY TEAROOM

Southend, Campbeltown
PA28 6RW
Argyll & Bute
+44 (0)1586 830 221
muneroy.co.uk

This tearoom is a wee gem. Based in Southend on the Kintyre Peninsula, not far from Dunaverty Beach, this is a must-stop if you are in the area. Built in the 1940s with its charming character and homely front room feel. The menu offers up traditional hearty homecooked meals and tasty sandwiches amongst other things. But let's be honest, this isn't your reason for visiting. Your reason is to sample some of the best cakes and homebaking in the land. Calorie counters and savoury tooths need not apply, as the portions are generous and worth saving space for! Not to mention their incredible sized meringues. This is Scottish hospitality at its finest.

235 **PORTSOY COFFEE SHOP & BISTRO**

2 South High St
Portsoy
AB45 2NT
North
+44 (0)1261 842 804

Everything is made from scratch in this little quaint cafe. Tucked away, this is a well-worth find. Great selection of savoury or sweet treats. What makes this place is the warm welcome you get from the staff.

Bars for a decent **COFFEE**

236 LITTLE FITZROY COFFEE

46 Easter Road
Edinburgh
EH7 5RG
+44 (0)131 659 5161
littlefitzroy.coffee

New to the Edinburgh's cult coffee scene, Catherine and Lychee will make you feel very welcome in their cosy cafe. Originally hailing from Australia, Catherine can talk coffee and will sort you out with something to suit your taste. Open from 7 am, it's a delight for commuters and early risers alike.

237 WILLIAMS & JOHNSON COFFEE CO.

3 Waverley Bridge
Edinburgh
EH1 1BQ
+44 (0)7542 974 642
williamsand johnson.com

Williams & Johnson roast some of the best – if not the best – coffee in Edinburgh. Their original cafe in Custom Wharf, Leith is a very cool place to hang out and enjoy the full experience of the space. Keep an eye out for their unique creative events. If you are in a hurry, check out their sister shop in Princes Street Waverley Store, ideal for a quick coffee if venturing off on the train.

238 CAIRNGORM COFFEE

41-A Frederick St
Edinburgh
EH2 1EP
+44 (0)131 629 1420
cairngormcoffee.com

Their coffee beans are roasted in the Highlands of Scotland and the coffee they produce is as special as the hills the cafe is named after. Make sure to keep an eye out as you can easily walk past the Frederick Street entrance, which is down and out the way. The coffee, the grilled cheese and the overall cafe experience are excellent here.

239 STEAMPUNK COFFEE

AT: THE WAREHOUSE
49-A Kirk Ports
North Berwick
EH39 4HL
Lothians
+44 (0)1620 893 030
steampunkcoffee.com

If you are into coffee then you are going to enjoy the Steampunk experience. Their single origin beans are ethically sourced and roasted on site in their converted joinery warehouse. The space is tastefully decorated with mix-and-match secondhand comfy furniture and the vintage bike by the entrance is also a nice touch. You can watch the knowledgeable staff roasting their beans from the cafe, and they are more than happy to talk you through what coffee is available and what might suit your taste. The soups with organic homemade bread are great after a windswept beach walk or – if the weather is nice – you can sit outside on the cobbled terrace. The retail space offers a great range of their coffee and equipment to get you up and running as a professional home barista, or if you fancy you can even enroll in one of their classes.

240 **SLAUGHTERHOUSE COFFEE**

Marine Terrace North
Cromarty
IV11 8YL
Highlands & Islands
+44 (0)7809 446 555

Right on the jetty of the Cromarty to Nigg ferry, this little unassuming shed packs a punch inside. Serving up speciality barista coffee and amazing brownies. The outside seating provides amazing vistas over the Cromarty Firth, which is famous for its dolphin spotting. Such a delight.

239 **STEAMPUNK COFFEE**

241 NO 1 PEEBLES ROAD

1 Peebles Road
Innerleithen
EH44 6QX
Scottish Borders
+44 (0)1896 830 873
no1peeblesroad.coffee

This is an awesome coffee stop if you are in the Scottish Borders. Serving up North Berwick's Steampunk Coffee in a cosy country-feel cafe. They also serve up some great cakes. A popular hang-out with the cycling community and a perfect place for a caffeine fix before or after your ride.

242 HABITAT CAFE

1 The Square
Aberfeldy
PH15 2DD
Highlands & Islands
+44 (0)1887 822 944
habitatcafe.co.uk

The Habitat Cafe is an absolute gem of a find in Aberfeldy. Serving up some of the best speciality coffee, with highly knowledgeable staff, this cafe is a destination in itself! The food menu isn't pretentious and is tasty and fresh. The grown-up sausage roll is definitely worth a shot, as are their cakes. Not to mention Dundee's 71 Brewing on tap if you're looking for something stronger. All of this combined in a lovely chilled setting, with a rustic feel, it's worthy of a stop if you're nearby.

243 POTARCH CAFE

Banchory
AB31 4BD
North East
+44 (0)1339 884 468
ballogie-estate.co.uk/potarch-cafe-restaurant

Situated on the Ballogie Estate, Potarch Cafe is run by the lovely Alice and Thomas and is a great stop-off if you are exploring Royal Deeside. The menu features fresh produce from the estate – nab a cinnamon swirl if there are any left! Another special mention is in order for the speciality coffee: Thomas was Head of Coffee for the world-renowned Allpress Espresso and his many years of experience are tangible in every cup at Potarch. There is also great outdoor seating in the summer and the place is bike friendly, which is a bonus on those sunny days.

244 CAORA DHUBH

Carbost,
Isle of Skye
IV47 8SR
Highlands & Islands
+44 (0)1478 640 666
www.caora dhubh.com

Caora dhubh – pronounced 'coo-ra doo' – means black sheep in Gaelic, and is a coffee-lover's haven on the Isle of Skye. Serving speciality coffee from Artisan Roast in Edinburgh, the wee space means that sitting in isn't an option, and drinks are served to go. Not to fret though, the shop is just across from Talisker Distillery and there is a nice bench or picnic tables for great views across the water and the island. And brownie points if you remember to bring your clean reusable coffee cup.

244 **CAORA DHUBH**

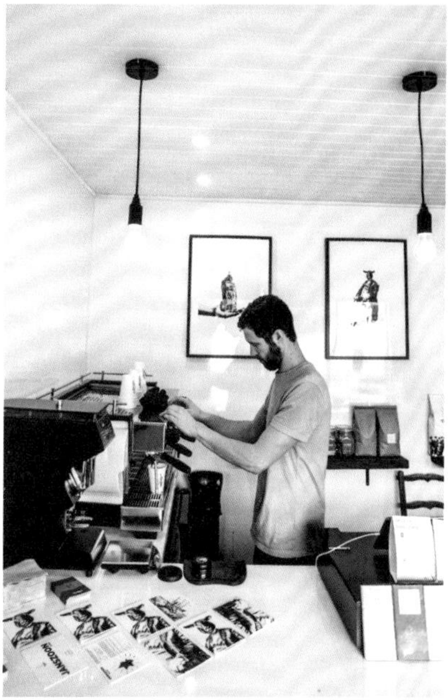

Police box TREATS

245 **CHEAP SHOT COFFEE**
NEXT TO: NICHOLSON SQUARE
Marshall St
Edinburgh
EH8 9BU

Cheap Shot Coffee is a wonderful little delight for coffee lovers in Edinburgh. New owner and barista Jordan is passionate about coffee and serves locally roasted Fortitude coffee in his tiny shop, which is housed in a charming old police box. Don't pass by without giving it a go!

246 **THE COUNTER**
NEXT TO: USHER HALL
Lothian Road
Edinburgh
EH1 2EA

Just off Lothian Road close to Usher Hall, you will find another Police Box serving great coffee. Popular with workers in the nearby financial district and surrounding offices, The Counter is a great place to grab a coffee on the go.

For WHISKY lovers

247 **BALLYGRANT INN**
Ballygrant,
Isle of Islay
PA45 7QR
Argyll & Bute
+44 (0)1496 840 277
ballygrant-inn.com

This family-run business is situated on its own two and a half acres of grounds and only five kilometres away from Port Askaig on Islay. The island is famous for its eight exceptional whisky distilleries and the bar – also known as Robolls bar – stocks over 400 whiskies. The bar has a pool table, darts and a wood-burning stove, which is great to pass the time on those inevitable Scottish rainy days. Bar meals are served for lunch from 12.30 till 2.30 pm and dinner from 6 till 8.30 pm.

248 **ARDSHIEL HOTEL**
Kilkerran Road
Campbeltown
PA28 6JL
Argyll & Bute
+44 (0)1586 552 133
ardshiel.co.uk

Just a 2-minute walk from the town centre this hotel bar overlooks the water and Davaar Island. Offering the finest selection of local malt whiskies, which Campbeltown is famous for, you might end up making use of the hotel rooms available. A short drive away is Machrihanish Golf Course, where guests can enjoy discounted green fees.

249 **DORNOCH CASTLE HOTEL**

Castle St
Dornoch
IV25 3SD
Highlands & Islands
+44 (0)1862 810 216
dornochcastlehotel.com

This 15th-century castle was converted into a hotel in 1947. It was once a school, a jail and a courthouse, which adds to the unique character of this hotel bar. There is also a microdistillery on site, where brothers Simon and Phil Thompson create their organic gin and whisky, which should most definitely be sampled at the bar. You can spot the Dornoch Whisky on the shelf as their unique labels stand out and are designed by Scottish artist Katie Guthrie. Tastings can be arranged, but booking is essential.

250 **QUAICH BAR**

AT: THE CRAIGELLACHIE HOTEL
Victoria St
Craigellachie
AB38 9SR
North
+44 (0)1340 881 204
craigellachiehotel.co.uk

This is a whisky-lover's paradise with over 900 malts available and one of the most impressive whisky collections in Scotland. Opened 120 years ago in the heart of the malt whisky trail, the staff can guide beginners or experts alike on a sensory journey. The cocktail menu is also not to be missed. The drams are not the only eloquent reason to visit here. Like the whisky the interior has taken time and skill to craft adding to the charm of this Speyside hotel.

LOCALS' *pubs*

251 **MALT & HOPS**
45 Shore
Leith
EH6 6QU
Edinburgh
+44 (0)131 555 0083

Malt & Hops is situated on the historic shore of Leith and feels like one of the last indigenous pubs left in this area. It's a cosy space with an excellent selection of ales and whiskies. Great in the summer as it catches the last of the evening sun and equally as great in the winter with its open fire. Head to Malt & Hops if you want a genuine traditional Scottish no-frills pub experience.

252 **KAY'S BAR**
39 Jamaica St
Edinburgh
EH3 6HF
+44 (0)131 225 1858
kaysbar.co.uk

This is a locals' pub. Once a Georgian coach house, it still has its original features. Stepping in is like stepping back in time, but don't let that put you off as this is exactly the point in going. A warm welcome from Fraser and his team add to the homely experience. No gentrified pricing here, their prices are as humble as their pies. Lunch only.

253 **PORT O' LEITH BAR**
58 Constitution St
Edinburgh
EH6 6RS
+44 (0)131 555 5503

The Port O' Leith has been an institution for anyone who knows this area. The stories and oral history to come out of this establishment are legendary and you get a feeling that these four walls have seen it all. The days of previous landlord Mary are gone but the spirit still lives on. Great vibe with loud music, excellent rum selection, lively locals and 35-ml measures.

254 **THE REGENT**
2 Montrose Terrace
Edinburgh
EH7 5DL
+44 (0)131 661 8198
theregentbar.co.uk

The Regent is a gay bar but open and welcome to all. The cosy interior and layout make it a great place to hang out, with a straight up laidback vibe. They have a good selection of ales, and cider lovers should keep an eye out for the Old Rosie on tap. The Regent is in a great place and often missed by tourists either going to Leith, up Calton Hill or to the Parliament. So be sure to pop your head in, you can't miss the rainbow flag.

252 KAY'S BAR

Pubs for a
MUSICAL SESSION

255 **CAPTAIN'S BAR**
4 South College St
Edinburgh
EH8 9AA
captainsedinburgh.webs.com

Definitely worth popping your head in at the Captain's Bar to see what the *craic* is. With folk music on most nights it can be a real treat. It is a small pub so wait around if you don't find the spot you want when you first arrive. Look out for the book swap near the musicians at the back of the bar.

256 **THE ROYAL OAK**
1 Infirmary St
Edinburgh
EH1 1LT
+44 (0)131 557 2976
royal-oak-folk.com

This wee, unassuming, warm and friendly pub is where you'll witness some of the best folk music in Edinburgh and Scotland. Hosting live traditional music every night, there's plenty to be had. Everyone's welcome to join in with the pub providing guitars, a piano and plenty of encouragement... especially after sampling their great selection of whisky and beer. There's something quite special about connecting to the culture through song and this is the place to do it. Don't be offended if you are told to quiet down by the locals as there are plenty of other bars where you can chat in Edinburgh. Etiquette here is to enjoy the music, and to get out of the way of the bar staff in this small pub on busy nights. Please tip the musicians if you can, especially if you request, they're not a jukebox.

257 THE BEN NEVIS BAR

1147 Argyle St
Finnieston
G3 8TB
Glasgow
+44 (0)141 576 5204
thebennevisbar.com

A piece of the Highlands comes to the hipster area of Finnieston with this wee cracking bar. Part of the 'Teuchter Triangle', including The Park Bar and Islay Inn – also worth a visit while you are here. There is an impressive selection of Scottish whiskies to sip away and a great choice of beers. Famous for its trad music sessions on a Wednesday, Thursday and Sunday but they can occur any time, it just depends what musicians are around Glasgow.

257 THE BEN NEVIS BAR

Great STOP-OFFS

258 **THE PINE MARTEN BAR**
Glenmore,
Aviemore
PH22 1QU
Highlands &
Islands
+44 (0)1479 861 253
aviemoreski.co.uk

Run by young local couple Katie and Scotty this wee bar is a must stop-off if visiting Cairngorm Mountain or Loch Morlich. A decor with one-of-a-kind Scottish snow sports memorabilia and a wooden chalet feel make this place special. A fine selection of local beers, gin and whisky is available. Check out their cafe if you want a spot of lunch. Accommodation available in their Treehouse and Glamping Pods. Ski hire is also available during the winter at their Snow Badger Rentals below the bar. Try out cross-country skiing on the forestry paths nearby. You can also grab an ice cream and enjoy it on the beach at Loch Morlich while taking in the stunning views.

259 THE WINEPORT

Cladach
Brodick,
Isle of Arran
KA27 8DE
Argyll & Bute
+44 (0)1770 302 101
wineport.co.uk

At the foot of Goatfell (the highest point in Arran) The Wineport is a perfect pre-walk or post-walk pit stop. The large beer garden outside acts as an amazing sun trap and spot to sample the local beer. The menu offers up classic pub dishes that are sourced from Arran as much as possible. The Lobster Tuesdays have also been a catch....

258 THE PINE MARTEN BAR

260 FIDDLER'S

The Village Green
Drumnadrochit
IV36 6TX
Highlands & Islands
+44 (0)1456 450 678
fiddledrum.co.uk

A family-run bar and restaurant situated on the shores of Loch Ness, Fiddler's bar has something for everyone. Their extensive whisky menu, beer cellar and kitchen have the best of what Scotland can offer. They also have a coffee shop next door that offers terrific Scottish homebakes, so well worth a pit stop.

260 **FIDDLER'S**

Cool HANG-OUTS

261 **THE ALLISON ARMS**

720 Pollockshaws Road, Southside
Glasgow
G41 2AD
+44 (0)141 423 1661

You'll get a warm Glasgow welcome in this traditional pub. Join the regulars at darts, dominoes and karaoke on a Saturday night. Not to mention the pub quiz on a Thursday. Serving locals' traditional pub bevvy since 1884, you'll understand why 'People make Glasgow' even after a short visit.

262 **THE ROYAL DICK**

1 Summerhall
Edinburgh
EH9 1PL
+44 (0)131 560 1572
summerhall.co.uk

Situated in a world-class multi-arts venue, The Royal Dick was once part of the University of Edinburgh's Royal Dick Veterinary School. This unique space displays alternative and authentic items relating to its veterinary past. On-site Pickering's Gin Distillery and Barney's Beer microbrewery along with a varied menu make this pub experience extra special. Make sure to book in advance to secure a table.

263 **REDMOND'S**

304 Duke St
Glasgow
G31 1RZ
+44 (0)141 572 5664

Redmond's has a lovely feel about the place. Local to many who live in Dennistoun in the East End, you're always bound to receive a warm welcome here. Their revolving taps always keep the beer choice fresh and interesting for those who want it. They also serve a classic pint of Tennent's, which is made just down the road. Their menu however comes from further afield with must-try bao buns and pizzas. Great selection of vinyl records being played.

264 NAUTICUS

142 Duke St
Edinburgh
EH6 8HR
+44 (0)131 629 9055
nauticusbar.co.uk

Nauticus is the new kid on the block and a great addition to the Leith pub scene. A quick scan of their menu will give you a fascinating Leith history lesson, of this area's seafaring roots. You step into a dark but inviting interior where attention to detail has been paid, from their Harris Tweed bar stools, to the mosaic name in the bar and the ladder to reach the top shelf. It's stylish but not pretentious. Their cocktail menu is specially crafted with some of the finest Scottish whiskies, gins and liquors and they pride themselves on selecting the finest Scottish produce. Great for a casual drinks and date night.

265 HOOT THE REDEEMER

7 Hanover St
Edinburgh
EH2 2DL
+44 (0)131 220 0310
hoottheredeemer.com

This easily missed entrance leads you to a different world. Push past the Scottish mystic Meg who guards the main door and be prepared for a magical experience. The quirky interior, old cinema pull-down chairs and a retro pinball machine add to its unique charm. Play the retro claw game, like the ones you find at the arcades to pick your poison to be used at the bar in the creation of a cocktail to your taste. Perfect city centre spot for great cocktails and something a bit different. Dive in and make your wish!

Drinks BY THE SHORE

266 **TEUCHTERS LANDING**
1-C Dock Place
Edinburgh
EH6 6LU
+44 (0)131 554 7427
teuchtersbar.co.uk

Situated at the shore in Leith, this place is easily missed, unless you turn down the cobbled dock street. Originally the old ferry waiting room for the Aberdeen steamboat. With over 100 malt whiskies, 20 beers on tap and a great selection of Scottish gins you won't be stuck for choice. The menu is pretty decent too from mugs of mac and cheese to the epic seafood platter. The best part of Teuchters Landing is its beer garden with pontoon out on the water. When there's sunshine on Leith expect a well-formed queue at the bar. Great venue to watch the rugby. If you are feeling lucky ask to play The Hoop of Destiny.

267 **DRIFT INN**
Shore Road
Lamlash,
Isle of Arran
KA27 8JN
Argyll & Bute
+44 (0)1770 600 608
driftinnarran.com

This bar has a fantastic beergarden overlooking Holy Isle. You get the ferry there from just across the road so it would be rude not to stop in for a pint. The bar has a traditional nautical theme and if Scotland is playing rugby you will find it on the TV. Great pub food made with local produce.

268 THE MISHNISH BAR

Tobermory,
Isle of Mull
PA75 6NU
Argyll & Bute
+44 (0)1688 302 500
themishnish.co.uk

First opened in 1869 the Mishnish Hotel boasts an epic cosy pub in this famous colourful setting of the Tobermory harbour. The interior has a traditional rustic feel with plenty of local and nautical shipwreck artefacts that really add to its great character. The seafood menu is not to be missed with a great wine list to complement the food. For non seafood lovers there is an Italian restaurant open during tourist season if you get hungry after a few drinks. If you are up experiencing the Tobermory nightlife there is a disco every Saturday night.

THE DELL OF ABERNETHY

SLEEP

Sleeping OFF THE GRID

269 DOWN ON THE FARM

AT: MILESTONE CASTLE
Fraserburgh
AB43 6JY
North
+44 (0)7954 989 737
downonthefarm.net

Totally off the grid and on a powerful sea cliff setting, Down on the Farm offers unique accommodation. In its offering there are hobbit houses, a vintage rail carriage with wood burner and a harvest hut, which was once farm workers' accommodation but now a snug getaway. Come here to switch off and recharge in a rustic setting.

270 SWEENEY'S BOTHY

Isle of Eigg
PH42 4RL
Highlands & Islands
+44 (0)1687 482 414
eiggtime.com/sweeneys-bothy

The magical Isle of Eigg leads the way in environmentalism and sustainability with Sweeney's Bothy being no different. Bigger is not necessarily better. This bothy provides you with everything for a perfect retreat, with a wood-burning stove and outside shower. The design is contemporary with natural wood and stunning views out to the Isle of Rum. Come here to escape and immerse yourself in the island's nature.

271 PORT A BHAIGH CAMPSITE

Altandhu,
Achiltibuie
IV26 2YR
Highlands & Islands
+44 (0)1854 622 339
portabhaigh.co.uk

This family-run campsite is a little gem on the Coigach Peninsula overlooking the Summer Isles. It provides electric hookups for up to 26 camper vans and space for around 50 tents. The facilities are well maintained with a clean, warm shower block, Wi-Fi, washing and drying facilities. There is also a pub and small restaurant located in a converted old croft that has been there since the 1800s with an interior to match. But that's a part of the charm. There's also a pool table and an old-school jukebox that provide great entertainment when sheltering on *dreich* nights. Put that all together with the amazing views to the Summer Isles and a little port where you can launch small boats or kayaks, it's a lovely place to rest your head.

271 PORT A BHAIGH CAMPSITE

272 THE LAZY DUCK

Nethy Bridge to
Tomintoul road
Nethy Bridge
PH25 3ED
Highlands &
Islands
+44 (0)7846 291 154
lazyduck.co.uk

A converted boathouse amongst the old Caledonian pines in the Cairngorms National Park. Set within six acres of land with the Caochan Fhuarain burn flowing through and duck ponds at Badanfhuarain. Stay in the eight-bed hut hostel, six-person safari tent or one of their three eco cabins that sleep two. Chickens and happy animals roam around. Sheltered outside seating areas with BBQs and wood-fired hot tubs. You won't be disappointed with this little charming place to stay. A very intimate, off-grid and peaceful setting.

273 MARTHROWN OF MABIE

Mabie Forest
Dumfries
DG2 8HB
South
+44 (0)1387 247 900
marthrown ofmabie.com

If you fancy going rustic then Marthrown of Mabie is a good shout. Nestled away in the Mabie Forest, the composting toilets, outside shower block and wood burners are bound to give you an off-the-grid experience. Accommodation ranges from an Iron-Age roundhouse, which sleeps up to 16, native American-style tepees, a Mongolian yurt and a 26-bed bunkhouse. Great place to immerse yourself in nature and take advantage of their Finnish saunas, spacious wood-fired hot tubs and woodland surroundings. Camping available but no caravans.

NOT YOUR USUAL *bed*

274 **THE DUNDONALD**
6 Mid Causeway
Culross, Fife
KY12 8HS
Central Scotland
+44 (0)7747 044 886
thedundonald.com

This absolutely stunning B&B sits in the historical town of Culross (pronounced 'Coo-ris' not 'Cul-Ross'): a perfect location for exploring the rest of Fife. Dating back to 1850, the guesthouse has welcomed visitors for over 170 years, and that rich history adds to the character and charm. Now the stylish rooms are bright and airy and you can tell that every detail has been carefully selected to make your stay comfortable and stress- free.

275 **THE FOUR SISTERS BOATEL**
Lower Gilmore Bank
Edinburgh
EH3 9NY
+44 (0)7445 494 331
thefoursistersboatel.business.site

Looking more in place in Amsterdam than in Edinburgh, this boatel is a fun and unique place to stay in the city. Floating on the Union Canal in the Fountain Bridge area, it's a surprisingly handy and relatively central base to explore Edinburgh. It's got everything you need for an easy stay with fully equipped kitchen, living room and outdoor seating. Space for up to four adults and two little kids. If you're looking for something a bit quirky, basic, and different, then this is it.

275 **THE FOUR SISTERS BOATEL**

276 THE ALEXANDRA

AT: ARGYLL KAYAKERS COVE

Cuan Ferry,
Isle of Seil
PA34 4RB
Argyll & Bute

This 110-year-old ex-lifeboat has been given a new lease on life as unusual accomodation. It's situated at Argyll Kayakers Cove in Cuan Ferry on the Isle of Seil near Oban, where there is a small bridge connecting you to the mainland. This lifeboat has stories to tell. First stationed in Norfolk and used in the dramatic rescue of a 65-tonne boat called The Sepsy in 1933, she was brought north and now provides shelter again. Decked out with all the mod coms that you would need for a comfortable stay. Sleeps six.

277 BORIS, THE MILITARY POD

Kylerhea,
Isle of Skye
IV42 8NH
Highlands & Islands
+44 (0)1599 522 270
skyejeeptours.com

Once a military trailer 'Boris' now offers a unique glamping experience in Kylerhea in south-east Skye. The camouflage and tough exterior bear no resemblance to the cosy interior. Space for two people with two single beds, wee kitchen, shower and toilet is all you need. Get in the zone and do some army-style hikes in the beautiful mountain surroundings. Don't forget your smidge (midge repellent)!

Sleeping ON A BUDGET

278 THE BAXTER

5/2 West Register St
Edinburgh
EH2 2AA
+44 (0)131 503 1001
thebaxterhostel.com

Just off Princes Street in the heart of the capital and a stone's throw away from Waverley train station, this hostel is in a perfect location to get in amongst the life of Edinburgh. Above the Guildford Arms that serves a great pint. Inside there is a Nordic/Highland hipster-style of design. The space is well managed with even one of the dorm rooms having a three-tall bunk bed if you don't mind heights! Upstairs mixed dorms for up to 12 people, downstairs a four-bed private room with en-suite bathroom. Free breakfast of eggs on toast to start your day.

279 THE MURRAY LIBRARY HOSTEL

7 Shore St
Anstruther
KY10 3EA
Central Scotland
+44 (0)1333 311 123
murraylibraryhostel.com

The beautiful red sandstone building stands out from the rest at Anstruther's harbour. Formerly a library it's now been lovingly converted into a hostel. Many original features have been kept with stripped back flooring, a grand staircase, sash windows, cast-iron radiators and a decorative mosaic floor as you enter. Offering a range of private rooms, family rooms and mixed four-to-eight-man dorms. Warm and friendly common areas with board games to keep everyone entertained. Very affordable prices, don't miss the chance to stay in this unique set-up.

280 CLEIKUM MILL LODGE

7 Cleikum Mill,
High St
Innerleithen
EH44 6QT
Scottish Borders
+44 (0)7790 592747
cleikum-mill-lodge.co.uk

Originally built in 1877 and used formerly as a drill hall, court room, cinema and bingo hall, this building now serves its purpose as self-catering accommodation. Now split into two floors you have the option to book a room or book the building for up to 12 people. The Tweed Valley is famous for its world-class mountain biking and Innerleithen is a perfect place to base yourself to head out and explore. The lodge is set up to accommodate active outdoor guests with bike storage, drying room and laundry.

281 KINLOCHEWE HOTEL

A832
Kinlochewe,
Achnasheen
IV22 2PA
Highlands & Islands
+44 (0)1445 760 253
kinlochewehotel.co.uk

The Kinlochewe Hotel is a must-stop-off if you are in the area and searching for a good drink or something to eat. The menu has the best of the north-west to offer, with the produce being sourced locally, from Torridon to Gairloch and it has to be sampled. Accommodation is also available, ranging from cosy double and twin rooms to the bunkhouse, which is a great option if you are watching your spending. Put it all together with their friendly service, it's a great place to spend a night, or two.

ROMANTIC *stays*

282 THE HIDEAWAY EXPERIENCE

AT: BALKELLO FARM
Auchterhouse
Dundee
DD3 0RA
North East
+44 (0)1382 320 707
thehideaway experience.co.uk

The Hideaway was built with lovebirds and luxury firmly in mind. Their modern lodges are equipped with everything you need to wind down with each one having a sauna, wood-burning stove, BBQ, double hammock and a hot tub on the outdoor private decking. A great place if you are looking to celebrate a special occasion or just want a break from modern distractions. Local quality produce hampers can be pre-ordered such as breakfast packs, movie night packs or even lobster that you can cook in-house, so you don't have to worry about leaving. Adults only, so unfortunately the kids have to stay at home.

283 FONAB CASTLE HOTEL & SPA

Foss Road
Pitlochry
PH16 5ND
Highlands & Islands
+44 (0)1796 470 140
fonabcastlehotel.com

On the picturesque banks of Loch Faskally near Pitlochry you'll find this Highland retreat. Originally built in the 19th century for port and sherry merchants this hotel has been furnished with fancy decor and luxurious touches. The 26 bedrooms are sophisticatedly styled and modern with hints of its Highland location. There is a spa, a sauna, a steam room and a pool to relax and escape in. The restaurant offers fine dining with an achievement of 3 AA Rosettes. The lounge bar has a spot-on selection of alcohol to indulge in, if you wish. You couldn't pick a better place for a romantic getaway.

284 BARNS TOWER

AT: NEIDPATH CASTLE
Peebles
EH45 8NW
Scottish Borders
+44 (0)1721 720 333
neidpathcastle.com/barns-tower

This old defence tower dates back to the 15th century and provides a perfect location for a romantic escape. This one-bedroom self-catering accommodation is packed with charming original features. The coombed ceilings, wooden rustic panelling and freestanding bath in the bedroom are just some of the features that make this stay special. It's a three-mile walk to the nearest pub or shops in Peebles.

SECLUDED

self-catering places to sleep

285 **GREEN HOUSE**
Quarry
Glenelg
IV40 8JT
Highlands & Islands
+44 (0)1599 522 756
glenelg-greenhouse.com

This wee retreat in the rural village of Glenelg is perfect for a couple and offers everything you need to slow down and relax: from amazing views over the Isle of Skye from the bed and a bathtub at the foot end, to a cosy wood burner for those cooler nights and even a wood-fired hot tub outside, where you can soak and stargaze in the evening. The basic amenities to self-cater are all there, although the Glenelg Inn is not to be missed and only a 5-minute(ish) walk away. Added bonus: well-behaved dogs are allowed.

286 **THE GRAIN STORE**
Tomintoul,
Ballindalloch
AB37 9HL
Highlands & Islands
+44 (0)1807 580 709
balnedensteading.co.uk

This self-catering converted barn steading sleeps up to four people on the Glenlivet Estate near Tomintoul in the Cairngorms National Park. An open-plan living area is flooded with lots of natural light thanks to the tall windows. Great place to base yourself to explore Whisky Country. Dogs welcome.

287 THE GREEN HOUSE

Woodend Road
Ettrickbridge
TD7 5JJ
Scottish Borders
+44 (0)7824 776 385
hollinlee.co.uk

This extremely stylish ecohouse has a living sedum roof, cuts of larch wood cladding and oak doors. With two bedrooms sleeping up to four people. It has a timeless contemporary interior and is kitted out with all mod coms. You are surrounded by paddocks and grassy fields. Sit outside in the summer on the decking, make use of the BBQ and enjoy the peace and quiet. Explore the surroundings of forests, hills and rivers. The nearest pub at Ettrickbridge is only a five-minute walk away.

288 FIDDLE HILL COTTAGE

AT: PRIESTRIG CROFT
Wilton
TD9 7NT
Scottish Borders
+44 (0)1450 373 424
fiddlehillcottage.com

Escape here for the perfect couples retreat far from the maddening crowds. Some immense carpentry skills have been executed here in the building of Fiddle Hill. Using whole trunks of Douglas fir for the posts and beams has made this noble building material into something striking and awesome. With large glass windows all the way up to the roof bringing in bursts of natural light. The French doors let you flow from inside to outside. You can tell there has been a lot of love put into this building taking into consideration its surroundings and care for the environment. Inside you'll find a log-burning stove and roll top bath. The main bedroom is upstairs in the mezzanine area. Free pickup from Tweedlebank train station if you want to ditch the car and use public transport. E-bikes available to hire. Homebakes provided for you and if you don't fancy cooking you can ask for a casserole (homegrown vegetable or local beef) to be left in the oven for you when you arrive.

289 THE BROCHS OF COIGACH

191-A Polbain
Achiltibuie
IV26 2YW
Highlands & Islands
+44 (0)1854 622 368
thebrochs.co.uk

These properties are wonderfully unique, and the architecture is born from the Iron Age roundhouses. Inside is open-plan luxury, with amazing views over the coast, wood-burning stoves, deep baths, and even a sauna. The surrounding area is one of the most beautiful in Scotland, so you're bound for a memorable trip.

290 OLD MILL ON THE SPEY

AT: HIGHLAND HIDEOUTS
Boat of Garten
PH24 3BJ
Highlands & Islands
+44 (0)1479 810 835
highland hideouts.co.uk

The Old Mill on the Spey will provide you with a spectacular base for a group or family holiday. Sleeping 14, it was originally built as a corn mill in 1720 and updated to a saw mill in the early 1800s. Now you will find much more modern fittings, cosy furnishings and bedrooms ranging from a large master suite to snug plush bunk beds. To add to the pretty views over the Spey, there is the fishermen's bothy – a great place to get the fire going, get out the board games and enjoy some quality time. There is also a barrel sauna and a hot tub to sit and unwind in. What more can you ask for!

SPECIAL *sleeps*

291 **INSHRIACH HOUSE**
Inshriach
Aviemore
PH22 1QP
Highlands & Islands
+44 (0)1540 651 341
inshriachhouse.com

Inshriach is the ultimate Highland escape, that lies in the shadows of the Cairngorms and amongst 200 acres of enchanting forests and nature. Run by the lovely Walter and Lizzie, there is accommodation to suit all tastes. The grandest is the main Edwardian house, sleeping 17 and decorated in a stately but homely manner. Then there is the unusual and wonderful accommodation consisting of a cosy 5-metre yurt and a converted former fire truck that now offer luxury camping and a contemporary bothy. The most romantic however is the shepherd's hut, right by the March pool. It has access to the hot tub and sauna, which have been upcycled from a horsebox and an army trailer. Excellent. Pair that with swimming the Spey and a 'Channel 4 Shed of the Year', that now houses the artisan small batch Inshriach Gin distillery. This is a truly memorable place to stay. Keep an eye out for their music days, which are great *craic* and not to be missed.

292 THE DELL OF ABERNETHY

Dell Road
Nethy Bridge
PH25 3DL
Highlands & Islands
+44 (0)1479 821 643
thedellofabernethy.co.uk

Ross and Polly with their small family have created something very special at 'The Dell', which is an absolute pleasure to experience. The setting is tranquil and really demands your attention to slow down and enjoy your natural surroundings. The stone cottages are beautifully decorated and sleep from 2 to 7 people. The main Dell Lodge sleeps 10 and is perfect for special occasions, or multi-generational trips. There is a plethora of options to explore this stunning setting, like forest walks in the ancient woodland, mountain biking, picnics, and chilling out in a hammock to name just a few. The Tipi Sessions are a great way to experience carefully selected music in a unique setting. With open fires, excellent drinks, soothing sounds and great vibes. Go and relax.

293 DAIRSIE CASTLE

Cupar
KY15 4RL
Central Scotland
+44 (0)1334 657 136
dairsiecastle.com

Ever wanted to stay in a Scottish fairy-tale castle? Well, this is your chance. Now I know the prices can look eye-watering, but get 14 of your friends or family together, split the cost and believe it or not it makes it fairly reasonable. A site for the Scottish Parliament in 1335, this castle is surrounded by its own six-acre grounds and includes six stately bedrooms. The decor is what you would expect from a grand castle, but the bonus is entertaining in the great hall with its chequered flooring, exposed beams, long dining table and carved chairs. Put it on your bucket list.

292 THE DELL OF ABERNETHY

LOOKED AFTER *places to spend the night*

294 BETTYHILL HOTEL

Bettyhill
KW14 7SP
Highlands & Islands
+44 (0)1641 521 202
bettyhillhotel.com

Worth the trek to the top of Scotland to visit the mind-blowing deserted beaches and melancholic but beautiful landscapes, it's good to know that there is a decent place to rest your head. Originally a coaching house this family-run hotel will give you a warm welcome. They have comfortable rooms, a bar and a restaurant, The Eilean Neave. Chill out in the garden and soak up the views overlooking Torrisdale Bay.

295 WINDLESTRAW LODGE

Galashiels Road
Walkerburn
EH43 6AA
Scottish Borders
+44 (0)1896 870 636
windlestraw.co.uk

Built in 1906 this multi-award-winning Edwardian manor house is full of style and grandeur. You get the feeling that every detail has been paid attention to here. The six bedrooms have a traditional yet contemporary style. Originally built as a wedding gift the 2 acres of land and features such as a claw foot bath make this an idyllic setting to unwind. The dining is everything you would expect from a two AA Rosettes.

296 KNOCKINAAM LODGE

Portpatrick,
Stranraer
DG9 9AD
South
+44 (0)1776 810 471
knockinaam lodge.com

This former hunting lodge was built in 1869 and was once used as the secret meeting spot for Churchill and General Eisenhower to plan the D-Day landings. Nestled near the Port of Spittal Bay in West Scotland, its isolation adds to its charm. Thirty acres of well-maintained garden that stretches down to its private beach provide ample space for reflection. The ten bedrooms are classically furnished and provide an intimate stay. The elegant hotel menu offers a culinary treat where you can sample the 3 AA Rosettes menu.

297 ARDLOGIE GUESTHOUSE

Dalfaber Road
Aviemore
PH22 1PU
Highlands & Islands
+44 (0)1479 810 747
ardlogie.co.uk

Kevin and Kirsty are the epitome of Highland hospitality. Their lovely decorated guesthouse is warm, welcoming and an excellent place to stay in Aviemore. It is situated off a quiet road right behind the Strathspey steam railway and has great access, especially if travelling by train. The rooms are tastefully decorated and the bothy outside is a great self-contained hideaway. The talking point at Ardlogie however is the beautiful breakfast. The menu is extensive and includes dishes such as a Full Scottish, Loch Fyne kippers, hearty porridge, venison and eggs various ways from the Ardlogie hens. This is all served by Kevin in his kilt, aka the kilted cook! So don't forget to hashtag #ThisChefCanParty! Excellent place to stay in the heart of the Highlands.

AT HOME *far from home*

298 **SPRINGFIELD HOUSE**
AT: LOVE CAIRNGORMS
Main St
Carrbridge
PH23 3AS
Highlands & Islands
+44 (0)7976 000 481
lovecairngorms.com

Springfield House is a luxury yet homely getaway in the centre of quaint Highland village Carrbridge. The rooms are spacious, and the interiors have been carefully selected by owner Kim, making the place not just feel good but also look good. Little touches like the Technics turntables and vinyls also provide great vibes to your stay. Outdoor decking and fire pit for summer months and only a few strides away from the brilliant Cairngorm Hotel pub, where you can feed and water yourself if you don't fancy cooking. Epic spot!

299 **URBAN QUARTERS APARTMENTS**
26 South Tay St
Dundee
DD1 1PD
North East
+44 (0)7876 450 961
urbanquarters.co.uk

This building consists of four individual contemporary apartments from the basement to the attic. Each self-catering apartment is named after a famous Dundonian. All fitted with modern appliances. Ideally located just a 10-minute walk from the train station and the V&A museum, this neighbourhood offers plenty of options to dine out in this revamped area. Minimum three nights stay.

299 URBAN QUARTERS APARTMENTS

INDEX

COLOPHON

EDITING *and* COMPOSING – Lauren MacCallum
GRAPHIC DESIGN – Joke Gossé and doublebill.design
PHOTOGRAPHY – Sam Mellish – sammellish.com
Roel Hendrickx – roelh.zenfolio.com
and Grant Anderson – grantanderson.me
ADDITIONAL PHOTOGRAPHY – p. 221: Diego Almazan – p. 223: Lukasz Gasiorowski
COVER IMAGE – Crovie (secret 69) by Roel Hendrickx

The addresses in this book have been selected after thorough independent research by the author, in collaboration with Luster Publishing. The selection is solely based on personal evaluation of the business by the author. Nothing in this book was published in exchange for payment or benefits of any kind.

D/2019/12.005/10
ISBN 978 94 6058 2431
NUR 512, 510

© 2019 Luster Publishing, Antwerp
Second edition, March 2022 – Third reprint, September 2023
lusterpublishing.com – THE500HIDDENSECRETS.COM
info@lusterpublishing.com

Printed in Italy by Printer Trento.

FSC www.fsc.org
MIX
Paper | Supporting responsible forestry
FSC® C015829

All rights reserved.
No part of this publication may be reproduced, stored in a retrieval system, or transmitted, in any form or by any means, without the prior written consent of the publisher. An exception is made for short excerpts, which may be cited for the sole purpose of reviews.